Through Her Eyes

Through Her Eyes

Mother and Daughter Parallel Perspectives on
Love, Loss, Blackness, Purpose, and Faith
A Memoir

Malia Logan & Olivia Omega

QUEEN'S QUILL
PUBLISHING

Through Her Eyes

Copyright © 2025 by Malia Logan & Olivia Omega

Queen's Quill Publishing
Denver, CO
www.QueensQuillPublishing.com

Book Cover Design: Olivia Omega
Author & Bio Photos: Evan Wilder
Foreword: Virginia Santy, PhD

ISBN - 979-8-9924458-0-0 (paperback)
ISBN - 979-8-9924458-1-7 (ebook)

First Edition: May 2025

To Olivia's Mom and Malia's Grandma, Lonjane
and to Malia's Stepmom, Jamie

TABLE OF CONTENTS

FOREWORD

I wished for a daughter all my life, and that wishing was bitter-sweet. Sweet for the joy and love I knew a daughter would bring. Sweet for the special bond so many talk about, a bond I wanted to experience. Bitter for knowing the unique challenges girls and women face in our world; for knowing that to be born female is in many ways to be born into a form of second-class citizenship, mollified or exacerbated depending on one's race, class, sexuality, gender, and other identities.

When my daughter, Keaton, was born it felt like the truest, most sensical thing I could experience. Everything else fell away and she was the center of my world. For a woman who has always been a perpetual over-thinker, the first year of her life was a reprieve. I woke up every day and thought instantly and solely of her. I played with her. I talked to her. I strapped her to my body and we went every-where together. This singular devotion was easy and natural. I never questioned it, never thought twice about my decision to step away from my tenure track professorship for a year to be a stay-at-home mom. I knew I was privileged, in so many ways, to have that oppor-tunity and equally privileged to, exactly one year later, return to the job that was waiting for me. Going back to my out-of-home job was the end of our "going everywhere together". It was painful to leave her with someone else for 8 hours of caregiving but as much as I loved our year of being together every moment, I loved my auton-omy, my sense of self in the world, my value as a woman and a thinker and a friend just as much. And I wanted all the same for her someday, too. I firmly believe, as Evelyn Bassoff writes in their book, Mothering Ourselves: "The mother who relishes and celebrates her own precious life allows her daughter to follow her bliss." Feelings of connection and separateness are a central component of motherhood. It's a continuum--a lever we slide to the left or right like the volume of a song we are listening to, depending on the occasion, the time of life, the need. An ebb and flow. It's what I love most about what you'll find in this book: a sense of currents and time and amidst it all the things that hold steady.

Becoming a mother doesn't erase who you are as a woman or a person. Nor should it. Mothers have to fight against the narrative of complete self-sacrifice and erasure for the sake of their children. But if there is one thing our daughters need to witness, it's their mothers living full, rewarding lives. Let them see it. Let them watch your big, sparkly life in all its acts and intermissions. Watching is learning.

We watch how others mother. If we are lucky we are surrounded by other mothers every day. I have loved those times in life when the amount of mothers around me felt like an embarrassment of riches. Only now that my daughter is a teenager do I fully appreciate the play dates we had when she was a toddler. Those were all about sitting with other mothers, laughing, talking, sharing, supporting. As women, we often focus on helping our daughters find and develop healthy networks of friends but usually neglect to do this for ourselves. Let this book be a beacon for all of us who have strayed from groups of mothers to come back to shore.

Let it also be a call to look out for one another's daughters. As feminist philosopher Eve Kittay states, "everyone is some mother's child." I'd revise to more pointedly state, every daughter is the embodiment of some mother's greatest hopes and greatest fears. How can we help share that burden, abate that fear, and allow the joy to flourish? To all mothers: please look out for my daughter. I promise I'll look out for yours.

That promise lies at the heart of my friendship with Olivia. I feel like I've known Olivia for lifetimes. Even before we introduced one another to our daughters, we spent hours talking about the joys and heartbreak of mothering our girls. Olivia was the first woman I knew who talked about her daughter in the same rapturous terms I did. We connected over our relationships with our daughters--both our celebration of them as incredible young women and our desire to make the world a better place for them became the foundation of our friendship.

For the past decade, Olivia and Malia, Keaton and I, would convene when we could amidst busy lives and ambitious schedules. Despite the age difference between Malia and Keaton, the girls developed a bond. I don't think we ever met up without the exchange of books, pens, and journals as gifts. It's a shared language and devotion among the four of us.

I love sharing stories about my life with my daughter, and she loves it, too (I know this because the first time she purchased a Mother's Day present with her own money, she bought me a "Best Mom Ever" coffee mug and a journal with "Mom, tell me your story" embossed on the cover).

I often use stories to cope with anxiety, specifically to interrupt negative feedback loops. When my daughter was little and worried or afraid, a story--a real one about my own childhood or even a funny (and appropriate) story from my college years--worked wonders in resettling the skipping needle of her mind to a different, less stressful groove.

Olivia and Malia have taken the process of storytelling and story sharing even further and thanks to their example, my daughter and I have gleaned the power of intergenerational narratives and a sense of responsibility to secure our own stories for daughters yet to come.

Lucky for all of us Olivia and Malia have shared their stories, perceptions, and outlooks here. I continue to find wisdom and inspiration in their words. I know you will, too.

Virginia Santy, PhD

INTRODUCTION

Dear moms,

Motherhood has a way of ripping you open, breaking you down, and reshaping you in ways you never expected. It stretches you, tests you, humbles you, and—if you let it—transforms you.

When I first became a mom, I thought my job was to teach my daughter, to guide her, to shape her into the strong, confident, capable woman I knew she could be. And while that's true, what I didn't realize was how much she would teach me in return.

This book is a journey—through love (and hate), self-worth, identity, faith and all the wild, beautiful, complicated moments that come with raising a daughter who would in turn end up raising you. Through Malia's eyes, I've learned that self-love is not just something we demand our daughters to have—it's something we must work intentionally to embody for ourselves.

Because they see everything—how we treat ourselves, what we tolerate, how we advocate for ourselves (or don't). Malia saw how I walked through this world as a Black woman. And she learned from all of it—the good, bad, and messy.

If I tell her she is worthy, but I don't treat myself like I am, how much weight do my words really carry? If I tell her to never shrink herself, but I make myself small in rooms where I should stand tall, why should she listen? So, what do I expect when I repeatedly tell her she deserves a love that honors her, but I accept less than that for myself?

Our daughters don't just listen to what we say, they study how we live.

So, if we want them to grow into women who love themselves deeply, who demand respect, who walk in their full power, then we must start by doing it ourselves. This book is an invitation—to reflect, to heal, to unlearn, to evolve. It's a love letter to the parts of me I hide and that I'm ashamed of. It speaks directly to every mother who is trying her best, stumbling along the way, and finding her footing in real time. It's a mirror for the parts of ourselves we've neglected or silenced, and a call to show up in the fullness of who we are—not just for our daughters, but for each of us.

May we love ourselves the way we want our daughters to love themselves. May we refuse to put up with what we would never want them to endure. And may I rise fully into the woman I want her to continue to become.

As my good friend Virginia Santy once said,
"My daughter is watching!"

With love and imperfection,
Olivia

D ear daughters,

No one ever really tells us how to be a daughter. There's no handbook, no secret set of instructions that are passed down. And yet, from the moment we enter this world, expectations seem to settle on our shoulders like a well-worn coat. We are told to listen and learn from our parents, to take care of our siblings, to be the glue that holds a family together. We are expected to be the listener, the emotional caretaker, the quiet but ever-present support for the people around us.

And somehow, through all of this, we are supposed to figure out who we are.

Being a daughter is a delicate balance I feel—a dance be-tween duty and dreams, between love and longing, between who we are expected to be and who we choose to become. It is both a privilege and a challenge, a role that shapes us in ways we don't always recog-nize until we look back and see the quiet strength we have built.

Through writing this book I realized that there is a lot that daughters hold. A lot that women hold. We somehow carry the weight of the world, even as masterpieces still in progress. But I want us to hold one more thing—joy.

No matter your relationship with your mother, your grand-mothers, your aunts, your sisters, or the women who have walked beside you, I urge you to embrace and celebrate the person you are and the bonds you share. These women—flawed, strong, tender, fierce—are your pillars, lifting you higher than you could ever rise alone. Their laughter is a song, their lessons are a guide, and their presence is a gift. So, cherish them. Learn from them. Let them remind you of your own strength.

My mom, Olivia constantly showed me the power of embracing who you are—fully, unapologetically, and with love. She taught me that our strength is not just in standing alone but in standing together. She showed me the importance of connection, of loving and being loved by the women around us, of finding power in sisterhood. Through her, I learned that when women lift each other up, there is no limit to what we can become.

But here's the most important thing I want you to take away, as a fellow daughter, woman, and dreamer: defy the odds. Take every opportunity to rise in confidence. Bet on yourself. Chase after the fire in your soul! We are meant to care for others, yes—but never forget that caring for yourself is just as sacred. Hold yourself when the world feels dark. Gather your broken pieces and turn them into art. Laugh loudly. Love deeply. Put on your favorite song and dance in your kitchen like no one is watching. And most of all, never, ever let anyone dim your light.

This world is yours for the taking. Walk boldly, and never stop becoming.

With love and laughs,
Malia

INTRODUCTION

"I am closest to my mother;
when I tell my own story, I tell hers."
- Toni Morrison

CHAPTER ONE

Becoming

Olivia's Perspective

Paper bag popcorn was a staple in my family—a humble treat that held so many memories. I still recall the sound of kernels bursting in a big old pot on the stove, their warmth and aroma filling the kitchen before we scooped them into a well-worn brown King Soopers paper bag. That simple snack fueled our park days along with peanut butter and jelly or cheese and mayonnaise sandwiches, potato chips, and a large plastic pitcher of Kool-Aid, all packed and ready to go as we piled into the sherbet-orange Ford station wagon, the "Omega Gang" was off on another adventure.

We'd head to the nearest park in North Denver and play until the sun dipped low, whether in the blistering heat of summer or amid the crisp chill of Colorado winters.

As kids did in the 80s and early 90s, we worshiped the playground—the swings, the monkey bars, and even the spinning metal disc of death (a contraption so dangerous it was eventually banned after it literally injured thousands of kids I'm sure). We climbed, jumped, flipped, and raced each other until our limbs ached and our lungs hurt from laughter. By the time we were done, we'd trudge home exhausted, our clothes stained with dirt and grass, our hands carrying the metallic scent of old playground equipment.

And sometimes, as if by magic—or misfortune—we'd return to a different house than the one we had left.

It wasn't until much later in life that I realized those so-called "park days" were, in fact, *eviction days*—moments of upheaval that we, as children, could only interpret as spontaneous outings. We never knew we were being shielded from something painful. We never questioned why our home address changed so frequently.

We just ran, played, and came back to whatever new version of "home" awaited us, even that of a motel or shelter.

These park days were usually orchestrated by what I affectionately call *Fun Mom*. In our unique, unorthodox, cult-ish household, I had four moms, each with her own role and personality. *Fun Mom* was exactly as her name suggests—young and young at heart and always ready with a song or a silly game to distract us from the world's hardships, shield us from our chaotic lives, and protect our childlike innocence.

Even now, she is the wild, a free spirit who grabs life by the dancing shoes, demanding that every stolen moment of sorrow be repaid with joy and adventure. Over the years, *Fun Mom* weathered heartaches and devastating losses that seemed too heavy for any one person to bear. She truly embodies the Biblical phrase, *He turned mourning into dancing*—all it takes is a little bit of music and suddenly she lights up and the entire room she's in does too.

Then there was *Working Mom*, the one I spent less time with as a child, yet whose sacrifices I now understand and deeply appreciate. She was the version of my moms who was always hustling, always doing what needed to be done, helping the other moms keep us afloat.

And then there was *Stay-at-Home Mom*—whose job was perhaps the toughest of all. In our household, the responsibilities of raising us kids all under one roof fell disproportionately on her shoulders, compounded by the complexities of life with (and without) my father and the unique challenges our family dealt with. I've come to realize that the weight she carried was far greater than anyone could ever imagine, and for that, I am profoundly grateful.

And finally, My Biological Mom. Whom I owe everything to.

I have few memories of my mom from before I turned ten—a vague presence, as if she were there physically occasionally but emotionally distant. All of the adults in my family were emotionally unavailable. It's hard to recall the details of those early years, perhaps because of selective or protective memory. There was always something missing in our relationship; she was there, I suppose, but in a way that felt absent. I now understand that my mom was doing the best she could in a situation far more complicated than I could grasp as a child—navigating the challenges of our circumstance, the instability of our finances, the unpredictability of my dad, and the intricacies of raising children with three other women.

As a kid, I naively and nastily vowed never to become like her.

My immature, critical eyes saw her as out of touch and disconnected—a mother who was simply not the type I wanted to emulate. I declared to myself, *I'm going to have kids in my early twenties so I won't be so old that I can't connect with them.*

My mom was the old age of 29 when she had me. It sounds ridiculous now—a poignant reminder that teens often think they know everything, even when they understand so little.

Perspective, I've learned, is a mysterious thing.

Now, with a daughter of my own in her early twenties, I see even more clearly how misguided my youthful perceptions were. My mom, once an enigma of absence, has transformed in ways I never anticipated. The relationship I've carefully directed and intentionally nurtured with my daughter Malia—built on openness, vulnerability, and genuine connection—has, in a glorious twist of events, sparked a change in my own mom. Over time, I witnessed her blossom into a chatty, humorous, and loving *Zumba-dancing queen-ager*, whose newfound warmth, openness, and closeness with her granddaughter surpass anything I had dared to dream of.

The journey wasn't simple or immediate.

It took decades of growing, healing, and learning to let go of old defenses. Yet, in the end, I see my mom now—not as the distant figure of my childhood, but as a vibrant woman capable of deep connection, one whose evolution has enriched the lives of those around her and of the next generation through Malia.

Looking back, those park days full of paper bag popcorn and the sugary taste of Kool-Aid, were more than just playful escapes—they were laying a foundation of resilience, of shifting family roles, and of the complexities of love in a chaotic world. Every eviction, every new address, every bittersweet farewell to the familiar, became a lesson in survival and adaptation, shaping the woman I am today.

And in the messy, unpredictable world of family, I learned that sometimes, the most profound transformations come not in spite of the challenges we face, but because of them.

Becoming Malia's mom wasn't on the calendar. For a meticulous planner who'd always had her life mapped out, I was supposed to be in New York City climbing the ladder to become a highly successful advertising executive—not preparing for motherhood.

Like so many optimistic 22-year-olds fresh out of college, I expected the perfect job to fall right into my lap. I was ready to conquer New York and dazzle the industry. I filled out more applications than I could count, perfecting my *smart and charming* persona through a string of interviews that felt endless. And yet, the advertising agency where I'd been interning didn't have a full-time spot for me. I felt defeated.

But then—watch how God works!

A door opened.

I found out about a program that matched new graduates with global agencies for a three-month placement, a chance to secure a permanent spot. I didn't hesitate. I submitted my portfolio, transcripts, and letters of recommendation, and, out of hundreds of applicants from across the country, I was one of 50 chosen.

Fifty of us, all fresh out of college, with a chance to live and work in Manhattan, rubbing elbows with industry heavyweights, and launching our careers in one of the world's most competitive markets.

I was ecstatic.

New city, new job, new friends, new colleagues.

I was ready to dive headfirst into this new life.

The catch? I was newly married to Malia's dad, and I'd left him in Colorado to finish his senior year of college. My plan—or so I thought—was for him to join me in New York as soon as he graduated, and then we'd take on the city together.

Spending that summer apart was harder than I'd expected. We filled the distance with handwritten letters and long, heartfelt emails—those nostalgic tokens of love before text messages became a thing. They were filled with gushy sentiments, the ache of missing each other, and dreams of our future. We were so young, so idealistic, so sure that love alone could carry us through anything.

Those months blurred into late-night work sessions, mid-day coffee runs, happy hours, and the thrill of working on real projects—like creating the first online sweepstakes for the Huggies brand and recording a Coca-Cola radio commercial. Between morning sickness, client meetings, and deadlines, there were networking events and long nights exploring the city.

One night stands out to this day. What began as an average happy hour in Times Square turned into dinner at a tamale joint hidden away in the depths of Manhattan, then drinks at a nearby bar. That turned into dancing at a club and, eventually, another bar. Only in New York can you hop from place to place on a random Tuesday night, each stop an unexpected adventure.

I still remember dragging myself into the subway in the early morning hours, stumbling and laughing with friends as we headed home. The sun was rising by the time we emerged from the station, casting a soft glow over the city. I climbed four flights of stairs to my tiny dorm room, crawled into bed for maybe an hour, then pried myself out again to hop back on the subway and make it to work on time. Somehow, I felt like a rock star.

Looking back, the thought of doing that now makes my middle-aged mom body ache. But back then, those late nights with friends, sharing our hopes and fears, created a bond that made New York City feel like home.

Through every happy hour, no one seemed to notice that I never drank. No one would have guessed my big little secret—the one I discovered the morning after landing in the Big Apple, just hours before I walked into Ogilvy & Mather for my first day of work.

I was pregnant.

Pregnancy wasn't just unplanned; it was something I'd been told might never happen.

Growing up, I suffered from debilitating periods, the kind of pain that swallowed me whole, affecting school, work, even my relationships. After countless doctor visits and unsuccessful treatments, they finally settled on a diagnosis: *endometriosis*. I was scheduled for surgery with a clear warning—I might never be able to conceive.

The news hit hard. Even as I prepared for the operation, I tried to come to terms with the possibility.

When I woke up from anesthesia, Malia's dad was sitting beside me, tears in his eyes, a huge smile on his face.

"Everything's fine," he said.

"Our babies are going to be okay."

I was still groggy, and the word *babies* hit me like a surreal, almost mystical promise. In that moment, he wasn't just saying it to make me feel better; it was a declaration of faith, a vision of a future that hadn't seemed possible. By some miracle, there were no traces of endometriosis, and the doctors said I should be able to have kids without issue.

I laugh at this looking back—no issues getting pregnant, but pregnancy itself? That was a different story.

To help manage my symptoms before surgery, I'd gone off birth control and instead relied on the rhythm method—tracking fertile days and being cautious. The hilarity of this is that the rhythm method only works if you actually work it. Trust me! And, what are the odds that, on the one day we were supposed to be extra careful, we weren't?

Malia is living proof that timing is everything.

And that sometimes, our plans are not our own.

When I finally landed in New York and left LaGuardia Airport in a yellow taxi, I couldn't shake the anxiety.

I was late.

Late to the program. Late on my period. Nervous about whether I'd missed my chance to bond with the other interns.

My stomach churned with a mix of excitement and unease as we wound through the streets, the sounds of the city loud and unfiltered through the cab's open windows. We arrived at my dorm-like apartment close to midnight, and as I climbed into bed, sleep felt impossible. My mind kept circling back to the possibility that I might be pregnant, that I might be carrying a whole new life.

The weight of it sat heavy on my chest.

As soon as the sun rose, I got up, determined to find a pregnancy test.

There was no DoorDash or Instacart, no Google Maps to find the nearest drugstore. I simply walked out the front door of my building and took a right, hoping I'd stumble on something.

After wandering for blocks, I finally spotted a CVS.

I couldn't find the pregnancy tests, so I worked up the courage to ask the cashier. He barely looked at me as he pointed toward an aisle, then impatiently rang me up, his indifference adding to my nerves.

After one of the longest five minutes of my life, the test showed positive.

I took a second one just to be sure.

This one practically screamed at me *girl, I said what I said!*

I immediately called Malia's dad. Forgetting about the time difference, he was asleep, so I left a shaky voicemail. Then, I called my mom. When she picked up, I tried to ease into it, rambling about the flight, the program, the city—anything but the thing I actually needed to say. Finally, I took a breath and blurted out,

"You know how I hadn't gotten my period yet and you said it was just stress? Well, I just took two tests, and I'm having a baby."

Silence.

Her response was disbelief—the same tone she'd used decades ago when I first told her I'd gotten my period.

"No, you're not," she laughed, brushing it off like I'd just announced I was moving to Mars.

It wasn't until years later that I realized this was her own trauma response—her way of shielding herself from difficult news, difficult emotions, and difficult decisions. But in that moment, it stung.

I needed her to believe me.

I needed her to understand that my world had just shifted in a way I could barely comprehend.

But no matter what she thought, "stress" would be arriving in just under nine months.

What was supposed to be a smooth 40-ish weeks took an unexpectedly dramatic turn when, at 30 weeks, I went into preterm labor—on an airplane—during a Thanksgiving visit to my newlywed college friends.

By the time we landed, my mother-in-law rushed us straight to the hospital. After hours of tests, the verdict was clear: I was in preterm labor, and the rest of my pregnancy would be spent on strict bed rest.

What a wild, unpredictable twist.

Bed rest stretched into what felt like endless months—though in reality, it was only six miserable weeks. And unless you've experienced it firsthand, you wouldn't understand that bed rest isn't about lounging in bed, watching TV, and having people wait on you. It's a grueling physical and mental battle.

Every time I attempted even the simplest task—standing up to go to the bathroom or taking a shower—contractions would hit with full force. The medications made me jittery, shaky, and even more emotional than usual.

At one point, I begged Malia's dad to take me to the mall, just so I could, for one precious hour, feel like a regular human. He wheeled me around in a rented wheelchair, and I found myself staring longingly at the kneecaps of passersby—hoping for a spark of normalcy, only to sink even deeper into depression.

At 36 weeks, the doctor finally gave the go-ahead for me to deliver.

In a desperate bid to coax my baby out, I tried everything.

Several tablespoons of castor oil. The spiciest foods I could tolerate. Hiking my way through the trails and hills of Boulder.

Yet, each day brought a tantalizing promise, only for her to seem to change her mind—a maddening back-and-forth that had me shuttling in and out of the hospital. Some days, I truly believed, today's the big day—only to return home in tears, waiting for her to decide she was ready.

And I'm sure I made Malia's dad miserable, too.

During one particularly long, 12-hour hospital stint of "waiting for the moment," he sprawled his textbooks across the small guest couch, diligently studying for finals. It was his senior year in college, his last semester before graduation, and yet here we were, caught in the imperfect, unpredictable timing of starting a family.

The most profound lesson I learned through that tumultuous pregnancy and delivery was this:

My timing is not my own. My life and my body are not fully mine to control.

God had already chosen the exact time and place for Malia's arrival—before He even created the heavens and the earth. As much as I resisted the idea, the message was loud and clear: no matter what I did, the day she would arrive was preordained.

And God has a remarkable, even mischievous, way of working things out.

On Wednesday the 22nd of January, I woke up before sunrise, battered by contractions and unbearable pain. Ordinarily, this was nothing new by then, but that morning held an extra twist—it was my mom's birthday.

I had been waiting, *hoping* to delay the inevitable just long enough to call her, wish her a happy birthday without disturbing her sleep.

But then, my water broke.

Instantly, my body went into overdrive. I was already seven centimeters dilated which was confirmed at my last doctor's appointment, so it was game time.

When I finally called my mom, I wished her a happy birthday and added, "Happy Grandma's Day" with a nervous laugh.

She probably thought I was joking—as so many false alarms had ended with her heading home after spending the day in the labor and delivery unit—but this time, it was real.

I won't bore you with every gritty detail of labor, but let me say this:

I have never experienced a pain so intense that I literally wished I could jump out of my skin.

I spoke clearly and directly to God saying, *it's okay—just leave her in there. She doesn't need to come out...ever.*

But, of course, she eventually did. She had to.

And what a birthday present that turned out to be for my mom.

Since that day, the two have been inseparable, sharing the most beautiful birthday milestones—as if fate had conspired to create an unbreakable bond between them. One of the most memorable was my mom's seventieth birthday. She shared with me that, growing up, she never had an actual birthday party.

Well, we changed that!

I threw the most epic surprise party, complete with all of her Zumba and church friends. We filled the restaurant, and she was in utter shock—her joy radiating through the room like a child experiencing their first major celebration.

The party fell on my mom and Malia's actual birthday, and while my mom was celebrating 70 years of life, Malia was turning seventeen—the same week she had just gotten her driver's license.

As the party went on, Malia left early to go to youth group—with my car!

It was nighttime. Dark. Scary. And my baby—my just-licensed baby—drove off into the night without me.

At that moment, I realized something.

My heart was growing up.

Then there's round two.

Another chapter in my unpredictable pregnancy journey—one just as wild, just as painful.

Mr. Michael Gabriel decided to play the *here I come, but not just yet* game too, keeping me on bed rest for three months after I went into preterm labor at 20 weeks.

My doctors diagnosed me with an *irritable uterus*—a term that hardly captured the turbulent mood I felt. And ultimately how pissed off I was.

I foolishly believed that after surviving the first preterm scare, I could somehow orchestrate a plan for this one's arrival.

After all, this wasn't my first rodeo.

But once again, God's plan trumped my own.

We endured several more trips to the hospital, each time with the hopeful expectation that he would appear. And each time, when my contractions subsided and he stubbornly refused to make an appearance, I was sent home in a haze of tears and disappointment—until, finally, the day arrived when he was meant to come.

In a twist of fate as sweet as it was ironic, my son was born on his other grandma's birthday—a baby gift for his dad's mom.

That made me, hands down, the ultimate, most thoughtful birthday gift giver ever.

Becoming the mother of Malia and her brother has given me the most beautiful insight into the mind of God and the depth of His love for us.

I could talk for days about how motherhood has revealed God's sovereignty, conviction, grace, and mercy—lessons learned through sleepless nights, the incomparable joy of holding my babies in my arms, trying to explain to an inconsolable toddler that I only want what's best for them, and watching a teenager drive off with your car for the first time.

Each trial and every unexpected twist have deepened my faith, taught me humility, and reminded me that life's most profound gifts are not timed by our own plans.

Becoming is set to a divine schedule that exists beyond our understanding.

Malia's Perspective

When I think of my mother, I think of creation—fabric, thread, and the hum of a sewing machine in the basement. Whether it was in our own home or at Grandma's house, my mom was always making something. She was the mastermind, the one who made every magical, pink, and princess fantasy of mine come to life. She found the dresses, signed me up for dance classes, and never hesitated to twirl with me in the living room.

My mom did what every mom should—she fed us breakfast and got us ready for school. But Olivia played music from the iPad when she woke us up, and getting into the car with a waffle or something was a chaotic action movie. Everyone else got to school on time, but I'm sure their mom never stopped for donuts because we were already late. A snow day was exciting for others, sure, but in our house, we had a whole celebration with a video. Past any "requirements," my mom made every day brighter! I have no memory of when the world became more magical because that's what I was born into. It started with my mom.

But I do have a memory of the first time I got to meet Olivia. She had a group of friends that she would spend time with and sometimes brought my brother and me along. We would go to someone's house or a big park, and every time, it always felt like a huge party. A movie would get set up for us, but I got to see sneak peeks of my mother, who is funny. Really funny. Her laughter rang beautifully and distinctly, bringing me joy. I got to see her take off any stress and dress up with her friends, just like how I would dress up with her. She would create costumes and designs, and I got to see the happiness bubble inside her when she presented what she made before they got ready for another adventure. Olivia's personality became even brighter as she let her laughter and creativity shine, and I was in awe. I truly thought she was the coolest person I knew, and she also tucked me in at night with our sleeping serum. Win-win situation if you ask me.

There was a birthday party that my mom hosted for herself — very iconic of her. It was a party for adults, sadly, but my brother and I really wanted to see her on her birthday. Our dad drove us up to the clubhouse, and for a moment, we got to peek inside her world. There was a disco ball somewhere, back at the start of her disco ball era. There were multiple colored lights that shined across the room, but my mom's energy shined brighter. The smile she held was infectious, and the party was off the walls. She knows how to throw a fun party. Seeing her dance that night brought the widest smile to my face.

My mom was always happy and herself around me and my brother—goofy, loving, and present. But some of my joy came from the times I got the honor to see even more of who she was in moments when she wasn't directly in "mom mode"—like when we were with our dad, when she was giving a speech, or when she was with her friends and we were just along for the ride. It was amazing, to say the least, to watch her let go in a different way, to see her personality shine even brighter, and to witness others interact with her—the Olivia I had always known, now seen and appreciated by others too.

Her creativity didn't stop there, in those moments. My mom collected mountains of pictures from these adventures she would go on and turned them into videos. The moment became timeless, and she even made videos of me and my brother. The music choice was perfect every time, and I watched, mesmerized, as her smile floated across the screen. It was in these videos, more than anything, that I interacted with Olivia. She was a goof, like me. Her smile lit up her entire face, the same face she makes when she pulls together these videos. Her magic oozed out of every shot of her, and that magic was something I always wanted to be around. So, I cuddled even closer with her and proposed another dance party.

Beyond her role as my mom, Olivia shone brightly in the world outside our home, whether hosting a party or commanding a room at CU. My parents both going to the University of Colorado Boulder made it my home as much as theirs, and the car rides up to Boulder were one of many. Every summer, Mom had a speech at the school and usually brought me and my brother along. I brought my note-books, colors, and books, and my brother and I had the honor to sit in the room with the high schoolers she was presenting to. I remember the feeling of settling into my seat, looking around at the eager faces of students who had no idea how lucky they were to be in that room. She had her usual flair—red lipstick and a black and gold out-fit. She held us close before gesturing for us to sit down, and from the second she introduced herself, a switch flipped. Some were chatting, some scrolling through their phones, but the moment she started speaking, all distractions faded. A very awesome switch indeed.

Her voice would strengthen, her posture straightened, and an energy filled the space that was impossible to ignore. Her eyes would sparkle, her smile got even bigger, and the room would immediately quiet as she hooked them into her world. She made jokes—some landed, and some didn't. Even when a joke didn't quite hit, she would flash a grin and keep going, her confidence unwavering. She didn't miss a beat, laughing at herself in case the audience wouldn't. For me, all the jokes landed… as I said, she's hilarious. She took her audience on a journey with her words and shared her passion with them. By showing them how to stand out with their businesses, she was selling who she was as a person. The story came to completion with applause, and I clapped along with them. She talked with the high schoolers, encouraged them, laughed with them, and afterward, took off some flair to hang out with my brother and me. She could shift between these roles so seamlessly—one moment a commanding presence in front of a crowd, the next just our mom, cracking jokes and asking what we wanted for lunch. She never lost herself in those moments—she was just as vibrant, just as warm, just as full of life whether she was standing in front of a packed room or sitting cross-legged on the floor with us.

At those speeches every year, I got to hear more from my mother and branding strategist, Olivia. It was from those moments that I wanted to be like her in every way—to command a room with confidence, to speak with both heart and authority, to uplift people simply by being myself: passionate, proud, and loving.

From that speech, I've seen dozens, each more impressive than the last. Every time my mom spoke, I wanted to be there—eager to witness her wisdom and passion unfold once again. And even more than that, I got to see the people she inspired while she shared her story. I saw faces light up in understanding, heads nod in agreement, and minds eager to soak in every piece of knowledge she had to offer.

That was the party with my mom that never ended, and over the years, I got to learn more about my mom. She got goofier, and we got goofier together. The kitchen has seen a lot of dance moves, and the number of movie lines we've collected has allowed us to have full conversations with them. We have our own language, built from years of shared jokes, inside references, and the kind of laughter that makes your stomach hurt. As I began to grow up and my mom continued to nurture me, we were able to connect more and more. I started to live more life, and that opened up a space for deeper conversations with each other. Past the laughs and movie nights, I could ask for advice and get her outlook on my world. In a unique way, my mom became my friend. The house sort of felt like a twenty-four-hour sleepover, talking about my school crush and laughing about it moments later. It wasn't just that she listened; it was that she understood, responding with the perfect mix of wisdom and humor. I got to see more of my mom's personality and learn more about her life as she guided me through mine, and past just being my mom, Olivia became a woman whom I looked up to and felt supported by in every area.

Over time, our conversations got longer, laughter got louder, and tears were shed more often. My mom became one of the few people in my life I felt I could be fully myself around, and I could tell her anything. Past any mom duties or "mom cards," I wanted to spend time with my mom, and her joy fed into mine. She wasn't just my safety net; she was my home. Her direction was soft, and her comfort was strong. There was plenty of advice that I didn't want to hear, even today, but I could see the intentions in what she was telling me to do. She knew better, or as I like to say when I call her, "all-knowing," but it was more than that. As I got older, my mom got more vulnerable with me, and rather giving me advice, she would want some. I started to see the woman behind the mother—the Olivia who had worries and uncertainties, just like me. Tears came from both sides, and I got to witness times when my mom didn't have the answer. She, at times, was as lost as I was. The path she would guide me on was sometimes the path she didn't take. One of the things I am most thankful for is my mom showing me where she has flaws and acknowledging her fears, sadness, or worry. Her strength wasn't just in her wisdom but in her willingness to be real with me, to share the parts of herself that weren't perfectly put together. As I got to my high school years, allowing herself to lean on me gave me a space to lean on her.

I could talk about my mom forever, and anyone who knows me knows that I will bring her up and brag anytime I get the chance. I never got to the phase of not wanting to hang out with my mom, and when I'm not with her, all I want to be is with her. I grew up assuming this was normal, that every daughter had this kind of bond with their mother. Why wouldn't someone like their mom? But through high school and college, I started to meet people—girls—who didn't like their mothers. Girls who didn't talk to them as often as I did, were distant from them, or didn't dance like crazy people in the kitchen. It was jarring at first, this realization that not every mother-daughter relationship was like ours. I found myself limiting my conversation about Christmas cookies with my mom while interacting with girls who didn't want to go home or didn't know how to tell their mom what they were feeling. It made me ache for them, for the laughter and comfort they might never get to experience. The varying relationships daughters have with their mothers didn't make sense to me, and truth be told, it breaks my heart. But it also deepened my gratitude. The friendship I share with my mom isn't just special—it's rare, a gift I cherish more with each passing year.

That deep bond we share is not just something unique to us—it's part of a legacy of love and creativity that began long before me. A big part of the creativity my mom shared with me, I also see through her mom—my grandma. Just as much was made at my mom's house as at my grandma's. If you needed anything, it was there: fabric, beads, crazy scissors—the works. Their homes weren't just places to live; they were places to create, to make something out of nothing. My grandma is incredibly creative and funny, always ready with a joke or an idea, but growing up with my mom, I started to notice something interesting.

My mom and grandma don't talk like my mom and I do.

They love each other deeply—there's no question about that—but their relationship looks very different. Where my mom and I fill a room with conversation, laughter, and long-winded stories, she and my grandma don't do that. It took having conversations with my mom to understand why our relationships don't look the same. The love and the way they communicated were dissimilar to ours, and there wasn't a lot of vulnerability for my mom and grandma. While my mom and I talk all the time, like never stopping, they just didn't. My mom can't go to her mom in the same way that I can, and the distance they made way back then is what was supposed to be the space for all the emotions and experiences. It's made interacting with my grandma complex, as my relationship with her looks different from both the models presented to me, past and present.

I love creating things with my grandma, and I call her whenever I need help with something. We've done many projects together, and putting something together for Christmas or a birthday became quality time for us. Early on, it became an unwritten tradition to call my grandma and tell her all about the day's events. She's the person I can talk to for hours, and she can do the same with me. Our calls are never less than an hour, creating space over the phone to listen to each other. Back in middle school, there were several shows that we would watch together, and still do. And if I want to bake a sweet treat, the mix is already over there.

The relationship I have with her grows day by day and evolves as my grandma watches me and my mom. They both watch, seeing a relationship that they didn't know. I get reminded of the gift we share every day, as my own mom didn't even have the same relationship that I have gained. As close as the three of us are, a lot separates us, and our dynamic consists of layers of creation, love, stories, and so much we want to say. Some of it gets said, and the rest of it doesn't. Or didn't. But the highs far outweigh the lows, and there is one thing that I love to share with my grandma, something that connects all three of us.

My grandma and I share the same birthday.

A very special day that I don't think we talk about as much, a day that connects all of us in a very beautiful way. It's a mother-daughter relationship being passed down, continuing a bond that is sacred and expressed in different ways. Over the years, including this birthday, I've seen that my mom and grandma's relationship is a love expressed in action, in the way my grandma immediately jumps in to help sew something if my mom needs help, or the way my mom is the first person there if my grandma needs something. Their bond may not be built on constant words, but it's built on something just as strong—unspoken understanding. That's something I didn't fully appreciate until we planned the surprise party. Well, and by "we," I mean my mom.

When my grandma's seventieth birthday was coming up, it was a big deal. We wanted to celebrate my grandma, of course, but my mom wanted to make it super special. She wanted my grandma to be celebrated by all the people who knew and loved her. My grandma lives in a nice house by herself, a place I like to call "Hotel de Grandma" when family comes into town. Sometimes the house is quiet, and my mom and I weren't over there as much as we could be to spend time with her. So, as soon as my mom told me the idea of a surprise party, I was thrilled. I personally felt that it was very important we show Grandma how much we see her, love her, and appreciate her. Who she is and what she does doesn't go unnoticed, and her light has changed so many lives, especially for me and my mom. And for the day, I wanted it to be about her, not me. After all, you only turn seventy once.

I am not the greatest at keeping secrets, so the fact that I made it to the big day is a big accomplishment in my book. The sun rose on January 22nd, and I called my grandma like I always do. We sang "Happy Birthday to You," a sweet, sweet ritual, and we went about our days. I don't remember much about this day—my seventeenth birthday—other than school and the usual. I was mainly excited about my grandma's birthday dinner, only hours away. The plan was for my grandma to be invited to dinner by my dad's mom and another guest and to bring her to the restaurant where everyone else was waiting. My brother and I rushed with my dad to get there in time, all of us in anticipation of my grandma's reaction. Soon enough, she came through the door, and a chorus of "Cheers!" came from the long table as my grandma walked into a room made for her. A room that loved her.

I teared up as she did, my heart swelling with hers. She moved from person to person, holding them close as they wished her a happy birthday. Eventually, my grandma got to me, and I squeezed her tight.

"Happy Birthday, Grandma!"

I didn't let her say it back, not that time. She got a hug from my mom next, and I smiled even wider. Watching my mom plan my grandma's seventieth birthday, I saw the depth of their relationship in a way I hadn't before. The way my grandma would step in to help whenever my mom needed her was the same way my mom shows up for me—just in a different form. Some love is spoken in stories and laughter, like what my mom and I share. Some love is built in action, in showing up time and time again, like my grandma and my mom. And some love is passed down, linking generations in ways we don't always recognize at first. Sharing a birthday with my grandma has always been special, but now I see it as something more—a reminder that, even in our differences, the love between us continues.

Their relationship isn't like ours, but that doesn't make it any less special. It's a bond that has evolved over time, shaped by growth, understanding, and the ways they've learned to show love to each other. While much of it remains unspoken, there's a depth to their connection that is entirely their own—built in gestures, in knowing glances, in the quiet ways they show up for each other. The three of us share something rare, a dynamic that is uniquely ours, woven together by love and creativity. No one else knows or understands it quite like we do.

For all the ways relationships can take different shapes, I always go back to the relationship that I am most grateful for—having Olivia as my mom. She was my first dance partner, my first cheerleader, the first person who showed me that dreams—no matter how sparkly or extravagant—were always worth making real. To be her daughter is to have grown up in a world where imagination had no limits, where becoming wasn't just about growing up but about embracing the beauty in every step along the way.

*"Each time a woman stands up for herself,
without knowing it possibly, without claiming it,
she stands up for all women."*
– Maya Angelou

CHAPTER TWO

Blackness

Olivia's Perspective

My awareness of my Blackness didn't arrive as some grand epiphany or a single defining moment. It seeped in early, creeping into my consciousness through experiences that, at the time, I didn't fully understand.

Some of these moments I don't even remember firsthand. They've been passed down to me in stories—memories told and re-told by my mother, each retelling a little more incredulous than the last.

One of the first stories of my Blackness, or rather my rejection of it, happened around my third birthday.

My mother had one goal that year: to buy me a Black baby doll.

I loved dolls—lived for them, really. Like most three-year-old girls, they were my world. But every doll I had was white, because that's what was available, accessible, and most common. So, in her mission to get me something that looked like me, my mom and her best friend scoured every store in Denver and the surrounding areas looking for a Black baby doll.

This was the late eighties, before the ease of Amazon searches or "add to cart" clicks. There was no two-day shipping, no guarantee that representation would be sitting on a shelf, waiting to be picked up. But finally, after an exhausting hunt, she found one.

She was ecstatic, feeling triumphant as she carefully wrapped the doll—a symbol of identity, of belonging, of self-love—and presented it to me at my birthday party, surrounded by family.

She told me that as I ripped through the wrapping paper, my excitement turned to confusion.

I froze. My little hands gripped the box, my face twisted in what could only be described as horror.

What is this?
Why is this baby brown?
And why is it here at my party?

Without hesitation, I took the doll and threw her in the trash.

Just like that.

I did not want her. I did not want to play with her. She was ugly.

I wanted a white baby doll—the ones I had already seen, the ones in the store, the ones I had come to know and accept as the standard.

I don't remember this moment, but I don't doubt it.

Because that's how deep these messages ran.

The rejection of my own reflection had already been internalized before I even had the words to articulate it.

The next incident, the first one I do remember, would happen in first grade.

This moment had a name.

His name was "the boy in the green overalls"—at least, that's what I've always called him in my memory. He is frozen in time, forever six years old, forever wearing those same clothes.

It was the first or second day of school, and we were still in that awkward "getting to know you" phase. On one of the first days of school, I remember a boy wearing green striped overalls and a matching green polo with a bowl-cut haircut approaching me. He must've been about my age—six years old—and like me, he was figuring out this new world we had just entered. But his words weren't ones I had expected from a fellow six-year-old. Without warning, he asked, "When was the last time you took a bath?"

I didn't sense anything wrong at first. I took the question literally, as children often do. "Last night," I answered matter-of-factly, proud of my response. I thought I was simply providing the correct answer. But then he laughed, a mean sort of laugh that echoed louder than it should have, and said, "You look like you haven't taken a bath in a thousand years."

At that moment, I was confused. What was so funny? It wasn't about how I smelled, that much became clear. This wasn't about cleanliness at all—it was about how I looked. This was about the color of my skin. As the weight of his words started to sink in, my six-year-old brain couldn't yet fully grasp it, but something inside me shifted. I didn't know how to respond. How could someone who didn't even know my name see something in me that made him laugh—a part of me that had always been with me, something I had no control over?

Embarrassment flooded through me, followed quickly by confusion. I looked down at my arms, at the brown skin that had never bothered me before, and for the first time, I felt ashamed of it. I didn't want to be different. I wanted to blend in, to disappear,

I laughed uncomfortably, not knowing how to respond.

At first, it didn't register. But then, like puzzle pieces snapping into place, the meaning of his words hit me.

Oh. Oooohhh.

He wasn't talking about cleanliness. He was talking about my skin. He was saying I was dark because I was dirty. It was the first time I had ever been made to feel lesser because of something I couldn't change.

Some wounds fade, but they never really disappear.

That day in first grade stuck with me. The boy in the green overalls never knew the impact of his words. He probably doesn't even remember saying them. But I do.

Now it was Malia's turn. When she came home one day and told me a boy in her class called her the N-word, my head and my heart went straight back to that classroom.

Straight back to the boy in the green overalls.

Except this time, the words were harsher.

The sting was deeper.

I sat with my daughter, grappling with the weight of it all.

The boldness.
The audacity.
The hatred.

I wondered: Where did this little boy hear that word? Did he know what it really meant? Was this how his parents talked at home?

As I held my daughter, I felt something else, something unexpected.

Guilt.

Had I failed to prepare her for this?

Any parent raising a Black boy knows without a doubt that "the talk" is inevitable.

At some point, we have to sit them down and explain that the world does not see them the way their moms do.

> That no matter how smart they are.
> No matter how respectful they are.
> No matter how well-dressed they are.

There will always be people who see them as a threat.

We were prepared to have that conversation with my son.

> To thicken his skin.
> To lessen the blow before the world delivered it firsthand.

But Malia?

I had never thought to prepare her. I prayed that she would never hear that word again. But deep down, I knew the truth.

This was just the beginning. A taste of the hatred and "othering" she would experience throughout her life. And there was nothing I could do to stop it. Growing up, I thought my mother was being dramatic when she told me about the Black baby doll story. I thought she was exaggerating when she said she saw disgust on my face.

But now, as a mother, I understand exactly what she felt.

I know the heartbreak she must have had, watching her daughter reject herself before she even understood what she was doing. And I know the guilt she must have felt, wondering if she had somehow failed me before I even had a chance to begin.

Now, as I raise a Black daughter who is growing into a Black woman, and a Black son who is growing into a Black man, I see them.

I see their power.
I see their beauty.
I see their brilliance.

And through them, I see myself.

They are a mirror staring back at me.

And as I see them, they reflect me, and I reflect them...

I want to provide the best reflection possible.

Because my daughter is watching.

Growing up, I absorbed messages about what it meant to be a Black woman from nearly every direction—television, magazines, school, my own home. Some of those messages were subtle, creeping into my subconscious like whispers. Others were loud and clear, handed down like warnings or rules to live by.

But before I can even talk about what that felt like, I need to give some context about my upbringing.

My mom and her mom are Black. But my three other moms? They are white.

As a little kid, I always wondered how exactly that happened. Was that intentional on my dad's part? Was that just how things unfolded? I never really asked. But what it ended up meaning for me was this: I was my mother's only biological child, which also meant I was the only full Black child in my house.

And you might think, *okay, but if the rest of your siblings were half Black, half white, what difference did it make?*

It made all the difference.

I was the darkest. I had the kinkiest, coarsest, stubborn hair. I also had the shortest hair. And I was in a world where I desperately wanted to blend in, to be just like everyone else, to look like the white girls at school with their shiny, flowing blonde hair and bright blue eyes. So, coming home didn't offer much relief.

Because home felt like more of the same.

I was surrounded by everyone who I sadly thought were prettier than me.

At least, that's how it felt. This sounds awful to say out loud, but it's the truth.

As a Black girl in a white world, I didn't just feel different—I felt less than. I felt like I would never be quite as attractive, never quite as smart, never quite as talented, liked, or popular.

Growing up, Black wasn't beautiful.

And it would be years before I'd even hear phrases like *Black Girl Magic* or *Black is Beautiful*, before those ideas would be celebrated in the mainstream, before self-acceptance and self-love would be talked about in a way that could have reached me.

For a long time, I just wanted to shrink myself down, to blend into the background.

But that wasn't an option.

Not when your Blackness is the first thing people see before they see anything else about you.

For years, I had an unspoken agreement with myself: *Don't stand out. Don't draw attention. Just get through it.*

And then, somewhere in my thirties, that agreement started to fall apart.

It didn't happen overnight. But one moment, in particular, stands out.

I had been working with a client, doing brand strategy, when I got the opportunity to attend a creative conference for women.

This wasn't just any conference. This was the most beautifully curated, Pinterest-worthy, aesthetically immaculate experience I had ever seen in my life. Everything about it screamed luxury, creativity, feminine energy, and success.

I remember sitting there, completely in awe, thinking:

I want to be a speaker at this conference one day.

It felt like a far-fetched dream at the time.

I mean, sure, I had built a career in branding. I had worked in marketing, advertising, and communications. I had experience.

But could I see myself on that stage? Could I imagine myself standing in front of that audience?

Not yet.

But as God would have it, life started shifting in ways I couldn't have predicted.

Within a year, I had reluctantly left my job and started my own marketing firm.

Some people would say I was brave. That quitting my job to go full force into entrepreneurship was a bold, fearless move.

But the truth?

It wasn't some glamorous leap of faith. It was out of necessity. It was out of pressure. It was out of the very real feeling that I didn't have a choice but to make it work.

That following year, the conference opened applications for speakers.

And I applied. And I got in.

But here was the catch: speakers had to pay their own way—airfare, hotel, food, all expenses covered out of pocket—just for the opportunity to speak in front of an audience.

This meant I had to be strategic. I had to make sure it was worth it. And for the first time, I saw my Blackness as an asset.

I knew from attending the previous year that the majority of the women in that room—nearly all of them—were white.

Which meant I had two options:

Try to blend in like I had always done. Or stand out on purpose. I chose option two.

Months before the conference, I started putting myself out there. Leaning in to take up space.

I created engaging content online, talking about my expertise and sharing who I was. I leveraged hashtags, tagged other speakers, created conversations, and even talked about what I was going to wear and bring. I built buzz and momentum before I even stepped off the plane.

And when I finally arrived at the airport, something happened that I never expected.

I heard someone yell my name. I turned around—and had no idea who this woman was.

But she knew who I was. Because of the content I had posted.

It worked.

That first moment in the airport was only the beginning.

When I walked into the ballroom on the first day of the conference, it happened again. During the keynote session, several people recognized me. Because they had been following me online. Because I was the only Black woman in the room. There have been so many moments like this in my life—where being the only one in the room was both a powerful advantage and a painful reality. Being the only one can be a good thing. It can mean you're memorable. It can mean you stand out. It can mean you open doors for others to follow.

But it can also be lonely.

It can be isolating.

It can make you feel like you're attempting to carry something heavier than yourself.

I didn't always realize it, but I tend to wear my Blackness like a pair of super thick Coke-bottle glasses. It colors how I see the world—how I see every space I enter, every experience I have, every interaction I navigate.

And sometimes, those glasses blur my vision.

And sometimes, they blur the vision of others when they look at me.

What surprised me most was when I realized that Malia doesn't wear the same prescription I do. While her actual vision is way worse than mine, she doesn't wear the Blackness glasses like I do. She moves through the world without carrying that weight.

And I love that for her.

I pray she never loses that freedom. Because the world will try to make her put those glasses on. And I just hope she resists it for as long as she can.

Raising a Black daughter and a Black son, I see them in a special way.

And through them, I finally see myself.

They are my mirror.

And as they reflect me, and I reflect them, I want to make sure I provide the best view possible.

Because my daughter is watching.

There have been several times in my life where I've needed to advocate for myself as a Black woman. Sadly, the need was there, but the courage was not. Too many times, I let moments pass where I should have spoken up, but I didn't. A reoccurring theme in my life has been this internal dialogue:

Don't rock the boat.
Don't cause a scene.
Don't make things more uncomfortable than they have to be.
Don't be an inconvenience.
Don't become the issue.

And so, I stayed quiet. I didn't challenge the obvious. I didn't call out injustice. I didn't correct misconceptions. This mindset—this fear of taking up space—became a major character flaw that played out in damaging ways in my work, my relationships, and my own lack of self-care and self-love.

But one moment in particular—one that still sits with me today—showed me just how dangerous silence can be.

During the last semester of my senior year in college, I submitted my nomination for the annual leadership award through the business school. This wasn't some minor recognition. One outstanding

student would receive this prestigious honor for their leadership contributions to the school and the student body.

My résumé and nomination were stacked.

No one—at least in my mind—could really top the level of leadership involvement I had. I had given my time, my energy, my ideas,
and my voice to shaping student programs and initiatives. I had spent
years making real contributions to the campus community.

I passed the first round of reviews and made it to the interview
stage. That day, I sat in the lobby of the business school for over 45
minutes, waiting for my turn to sit in front of a panel of at least ten
people—students and faculty—who would decide who would receive the award.

Forty-five minutes passed.

A young woman peeked out of the conference room, scanning
the lobby for someone. She didn't find who she was looking for. So
she went back inside.

More time passed.

She came back out, again looking around. Barely making eye
contact with me. Clearly searching for someone who, in her mind,
was still missing.

At first, I thought nothing of it. Maybe someone had missed
their time slot. Maybe they were behind schedule. But as she came
out a third time, glancing over me like I was a ghost, something clicked.

She was looking for me. But she didn't see me. Not really.

Not as Olivia Omega, the leadership award finalist. Not as the student they selected for an interview. Not as the accomplished young woman who had poured years of effort into the school.

Not at all.

Finally, I got up and knocked on the door. I opened it to find an entire room filled with white faces staring back at me. They looked confused, like I had stumbled into the wrong room. I probably looked confused because I had been waiting for an interview for forty-five minutes. I spoke, trying to break through their uncertainty.

"Are you looking for Olivia Omega?", I asked.

"Yes," they said.

"I'm Olivia," I said with conviction.

A look of surprise and embarrassment swept over their faces.

I did not look like a Black woman on paper.

And they obviously expected someone else.

They had been searching for a different face, peering into the lobby, scanning right past me, never even considering that the Black woman sitting right there, waiting, invisible, was the one they were looking for.

I walked into that room, sat down, and did my interview. I answered their questions. I spoke about my experiences. I held my head high. But the entire time, I was holding back tears.

Because the truth was obvious. They had already judged me. Before I even opened my mouth. Before I even walked through that door. And I had seen it happen in real-time. But I pushed through, because I had earned my spot there.

We finally got to graduation day.

The commencement ceremony was a blur of caps and gowns, of speeches and polite applause. I was one of only three Black students receiving bachelor's degrees that day.

They got to the moment in the program where they would announce the recipient of the University of Colorado Boulder Leeds School of Business Leadership Award.

They started listing the achievements of the recipient, and I had pretty much checked out.

Just give me my cheap degree holder thing so we can keep it moving.

And then, I heard it.

"The award goes to… Olivia Omega."

Wait. What?

You mean to tell me that after all of that, after being ignored in the lobby, after being looked over in plain sight, after them not even considering I could be the one they were looking for...

I got the award? You've got to be kidding.

If there was ever a lesson in not judging a book by its cover, this was it.

But let's be real. People do it.

We always have. And we always will.

The world hasn't changed much since then, but I have seen a shift—a movement of women embracing the beauty of their Blackness, a rising appreciation for what it means to take up space, a new way of loving and celebrating who we are.

And the most beautiful example of that?

My daughter, Malia.

Malia's outward expression of self-love has been present since day one.

As a young girl, she didn't just identify as Black.

She identified as Malia.

> Bold.
> Expressive.
> Dramatic.
> Passionate.

She is a living, breathing example of what it means to move freely through the world, to not shrink yourself, to not let the world decide your worth.

A freedom that I wish I had.

A freedom that I am still learning to claim for myself.

Hair plays a huge role in the journey, identity, and self-acceptance of Black women. It carries history, culture, beauty, and at times, burden. And for me, hair always seemed to be everything.

From a young age, I was conditioned to believe that long, straight, and silky was the ultimate goal. Around seven years old, my mom relaxed my hair for the first time—to make it straighter, less kinky, easier to manage. I remember the horrible smell of the chemicals, that sharp burning sensation on my scalp, the countdown until it was time to rinse before my skin would literally start melting off.

It was toxic.
And it was addicting.

Because the moment I saw my hair moving and flowing, I thought, *This is what pretty looks like.*

My goal from then on was to grow it long—long like my sisters'. Long like the girls at school. Long like the images of beauty I saw everywhere except in my own mirror.

And for years, I kept up the routine—the burning, the breakage, the dependency on that chemical just to feel "presentable."

After I had my first baby, my hair started to fall out.

The books and postpartum articles told me this was normal— that many women experience hair thinning after giving birth. But normal didn't make it any less devastating.

I had spent years growing it, protecting it, relying on it. And now, it was failing me.

So, I made the boldest move I had ever made.

I cut it all off.

I was almost bald, and for the first time since childhood, I saw my real hair—untouched, unrelaxed, unaltered.

No more "creamy crack" (a.k.a. chemical relaxers) for me.

I stood in the mirror, staring at my reflection, waiting for some big *aha* moment—some deep acceptance of my natural beauty, some liberating self-love revelation.

Instead? I hated it.

And if I wasn't sure how I felt about my new look, the men in my life had no hesitation in telling me exactly what they thought.

"You look like a boy," Malia's dad joked.

"Why would you do something like that?" my dad asked, truly baffled.

"Are you going through a midlife crisis, or just trying to assert your masculinity?" my brother inquired, with a tone that implied neither was a good option.

I already had my own struggles with self-image.

Their responses didn't help. At all.

It only took four days for regret to settle in.

And four weeks before I found myself back in the salon, surrendering to the creamy crack once again, desperate to undo my "mistake."

Years later, I would chop it all off again. But this second chop was on my own terms.

But this time, it wasn't out of frustration or desperation.

It was out of confidence.

This time, I didn't cut my hair because I felt like I had no other choice.

I cut it because I wanted to. Because I had finally begun to care less and less about what other people thought. This big chop wasn't just a haircut. It was a declaration. A statement.

A reclaiming of what beauty could look like on my own terms.

And as much as I had spent my whole life seeking acceptance, it was this moment—this act of self-liberation—that made me feel truly seen.

I wanted Malia—and every young Black girl who would ever struggle with her reflection—to know that beauty wasn't tied to the length of her hair. That she could wear it long or short, straight or curly, braided or shaved—and still be undeniably, unapologetically beautiful. That her Blackness was not a burden to fix but a crown to wear. That no chemical, flat iron, or societal standard could dictate her worth.

This time, I felt free—from the weight of expectations, from the pressure to conform, from the belief that my beauty had to look a certain way. This time, I created my own definition of beautiful—and dare I say sexy.

What's interesting is that it took becoming a mother to truly see myself.

My Black womanhood—and my identity as a mother—was affirmed by Malia as she grew into her own sense of self.

Watching her move through the world with such unshakable confidence, such bold self-expression, such pride in who she is, made me realize something profound.

Her views of herself as a young woman very much mirror my views of myself today.

> The good.
> The bad.
> The indifferent.

And that pushes me to keep loving myself harder, to keep celebrating who I am, to keep dismantling the insecurities that were planted in me long ago.

Because my daughter is watching.

And the best thing I can give her is the example of a mother who finally learned to love herself.

Malia's Perspective

I don't remember realizing I that I am Black. I suppose it was when I was very little, when I started to play with other kids—kids whose skin looked different than mine. Was it the day we learned our colors, when I looked at the flashcard labeled 'brown' and then down at my skin? I wonder if that was a cool idea—to see that I was a color. That I was a color and noticed that my friends were different colors. See, when you're younger, everything is pretty much black or white. Good compared to evil, what is right versus what is wrong. That is fair, but this is unfair. That is a truth, or that is a lie. But ironically, finding out that there is Black and White made everything so much more complicated.

Beloved Colorado has a lot of high points, and it is a place I am forever grateful to call home. But one thing Colorado lacked while I was growing up was diversity. To this day, "Colorful Colorado" somewhat lacks color. Living in a predominantly white neighborhood led to having white friends and white classmates. But let's pause here—they were not my 'white' friends or 'white' classmates. They were just friends. I wouldn't be shocked if there were moments I realized I didn't look like them, but that didn't matter. They liked *Hannah Montana,* I liked *Hannah Montana,* so that was all we needed to know! I am so jealous of younger Malia—of the time when skin color didn't mean anything to me. More importantly, when the color of my skin didn't mean anything to anyone else.

Before I could process my Black skin, I hated my Black hair. This wild, curly, tangly mane that usually fell haphazardly around my head. A lot of photos of me as a child feature my most recent set of bizarre glasses and my hair out and bold. In certain styles, my hair would get down to my waist, and all the women at church and other events wanted my hair. But man, my hair was a pain.

One of my first memories of my hair is sitting in the living room all day as Mom tended to the mess on my head. There's a possibility I'm being dramatic here, but I swore we worked on those damn braids from sunrise to sunset. If we were to contact my friends from that era, I'm pretty sure they'd say I never hung out on the weekends. *Sorry*, I would tell them, *I have to do my hair.* I picked my pillow in the living room, Mom told me where to sit, and I'd place my pillow accordingly and grab a book before sitting down. The steps were the same every time, and it got old the first time we did it. She had to take out every braid she had practically sewn into my head a couple of weeks prior, and that alone took multiple hours. My back would start to ache, and my butt would grow sore. On average, my foot would fall asleep one to two times in that first round of sitting. Nothing was worse than sitting on the floor all day long.

Actually, no, I take it back. Sitting on the floor wasn't the worst part. The part I truly dreaded occurred after my mom undid the final braid. Once my hair was released, it was time to remove the grime and dirt. I'm sure I asked her a million times why I had to lie in a kitchen sink to wash my hair, and while I don't remember any of her reasons, that conversation ended in a *"because I said so."* The epitome of the mom card, as she would like to say. For those of you who have never had to put your head in the sink, let me relieve you from ever having to experience such a thing.

When I was little, my mom set up a chair, and I carefully climbed onto the counter. In our townhome, I had perfected the art of fitting my body just right. With the microwave at the edge, I had to contort myself—first sitting, then lowering my hair into the sink, followed by my head, neck, and back. The hardest part was twisting diagonally, bending my legs, and tucking my feet beside the microwave just enough to keep from slipping. Cramped like a coiled snake, I lay there for at least an hour as hot water poured over my head.

The pain would never end, and the hot water kept getting hotter. Small talk was shared with my mom, but it never lasted long. Every time wash day came around, we argued about who hated the day more. I still think I hated it more, but let's wait until I have to wash my own daughter's hair. The ceiling of the kitchen cupboard would only entertain me for so long before I started to zone out, and by the time I was finally allowed up, my body had aged a decade. Popping noises would soon come from all over, and my hair weighed like stones that tried to send me to the kitchen floor. But there was no time to play or do anything else. Now, we had to drench the hair in heat. It would take hours before the blow drying and straightening were done, and afterward, we still had to put my braids back together.

Miserable is the best way to describe all of this, and I dreaded it every time without fail. Styling it every morning sucked the life out of me, and it still does today. But all of this is not why I hated my hair. My Black hair and I never got along because of what I would see when I left that living room and kitchen. Every time I walked outside and into the world, I got to visually see what I didn't have.

I saw it the most at my elementary and middle school. Out of my class of roughly sixty people, only ten of us were Black. As all the students filed in for homeroom, I watched as all the girls walked by with a "freedom" I couldn't have. All different colors, different styles, different crowns of hair. All of their hair swayed and shined, and I would watch from a distance, knowing that not a single set of hair matched mine. My hair—curly and wild, woven tightly into contained braids—was unique. *Unique* being the ideal word, from my head to my chocolate skin.

High and low, I would beg my mom, "I just want hair like the other girls." My mom would only smile at this—a sad smile, I think, looking back. All she could say to me was, "You're not like other girls." There are not enough words that God created to describe how badly I wanted to just blend in with the rest. The first time my mom let me wear my hair out—and straightened—to school was in fifth grade, and it was the best day of my life (at the time). Finally, I looked like my friends! I flicked my hair across my shoulder and fashion walked down the hallway like the rest of the girls, joy and belonging oozing out of my body. My smile broke my face that day, and I never wanted to go back to what was.

So, every chance I get, I straighten my hair. I plug in my mom's "blowtorch," and I quickly set fire to my crown of brown, crippling each curl until they're gone. The fire-licking relaxer presses down on each gem, and every time I feel each piece of my hair burn, more ruined than the last time. It's a decision I make constantly, yet it's anything but easy. Whenever I straighten my curls, I get looks—comments laced with judgment. Anytime something important is around the corner, I want my hair straightened—but friends, family, acquaintances—almost everyone—disapprove, which ironically feels worse than the heat damage itself. They'd ask why, and my answer never changed: *It's easier.* Sue me for being lazy; I'll plead guilty. Waking up hours earlier to tame my curls felt like a nightmare.

Straight hair meant freedom. But deeper than convenience, I felt more beautiful with it. Even admitting that now breaks my heart. Thinking I wasn't pretty with curls makes me sick to my stomach.

It took years—and writing this book—to understand why I resented my curls. Beyond the mirror, beyond my morning routine. In reality, I think I loved my curls, and slowly that love started to get chipped away. Something precious that I owned was taken out into the world, exposed, and it got tarnished. I wanted so badly to be like everyone else. To be pretty in the ways I saw reflected back at me every day—in movies, in classrooms, in friend groups. I thought if I could just straighten one more time, just brush my hair down enough, maybe I could "be that girl". The loudness of my curls felt like they were announcing something I wasn't ready to claim. So, piece by piece, I lost sight of the beauty in them. I stopped seeing the gift. I forgot that each curl was its own fingerprint, and my natural hair wasn't just something on top of my head—it was a living part of who I am. And still, I try to erase it, believing erasure would make me belong.

I spent so long trying not to be myself that, by the time I embraced my "unnatural," no one liked it. No one liked the hair I thought I wanted—after I'd wanted it for so long. And suddenly, all the people who once ignored my curls had something to say: "I loved your natural hair," "You should wear it out more," "Your curls were so pretty." Where was all that love when I was hiding? Where was it when I was burning it all away? I constantly feel stuck in a tug-of-war between who I am and who I want to be. Do I be myself? Or do I be who I *wish* I could be—the version of me they'd finally approve of?

My crown is heavy, and some days, my smile fades. Before I walk out the door, I'll pull my hair back, tucking it away. I got to witness my mom's journey too—her seasons of love and frustration with her own hair. I watched her chop it all off, wear it in glorious afros, pull it into sleek braids, and at times, leave it bare. Her hair told stories, too. Some of celebration, others of weariness. Some days, I'd watch her in the mirror—picking, parting, pressing—and see both pride and pain behind her eyes. I saw her fight to embrace what the world didn't always welcome. And even though she's the one who said, "You're not like the other girls," I saw that she carried her own ache, too. I wish neither of us had to feel that way. I wish beauty didn't come with such a fight.

But that's the thing about growing up Black in a world that doesn't always see your beauty—you start to believe the lies. And one day, the ache hits deeper. The moment you realize it's not just about hair or blending in. It's about something far more painful. The moment when being Black isn't just something you see in the mirror—but something someone else decides to use against you.

My "moment" occurred during what my school called Electives. In middle school, you had Electives as your last class of the day, and every quarter, I believe, you signed up for a new one. The same Electives were offered to the sixth, seventh, and eighth graders, covering a wide range of interests and activities. During my time, I did an improv class, a mural painting class, and a class where we were taught different card games. The only requirement for Electives was that you had to take at least one sport-related Elective and one art-related Elective a year.

At a certain point in sixth grade, I finally gave in and signed up for Basketball. Now, to be clear, I only signed up for Basketball because it was the sport that generally sounded the most fun with my extremely limited knowledge of all things sports. That being said, I had zero clue how to play basketball, other than knowing there was an orange ball and a hoop. But with my green and purple glasses and navy uniform, I would head into the gym and prepare.

I don't remember the crash course we got in how to play, but I'm sure the P.E. teacher did. From then on, the rest of the quarter looked the same. We would split into four teams, go to our sides of the court, and play until the day was over. Simple enough, short of the number of times I would get hit in the face and my glasses would break.

One day, I was put on one side of the gym, and this boy in the eighth grade was put on the opposing team on the same side. There was nothing special about him, which I feel the need to make clear every time I share this story. I didn't know him, and he didn't know me. He wasn't a bully—to me, anyway. He was just an older boy who was a jerk, and let's be real, all boys are jerks in the eighth grade. His name started with a C, I think. Let's call him Chuck.

That day, the whistle had blown, and I knew just enough to participate. You can't hold the ball and walk. Throw it toward the net-thingy. Pass to your team and block the opposite team. Soon enough, I found myself next to Chuck, who had the ball, and I knew one thing: block him, and if possible, get the ball back. I honestly couldn't tell why I even tried to get the ball from him, but I wanted to try this sport thing, so I went up to him and started blocking him. I blocked him well—too well. I should've let him go; it was just basketball.

I was up in his face enough that it started to stress him out. I remember seeing the sweat on his face, which was disgusting. He was looking everywhere but at me and almost started to get angry at me. But I held my ground, and it only took a couple more seconds before he muttered,

"I need to get away from this Black woman."

I remember stopping. He got away because I was confused. What was I? There were many things I had already known myself to be. A daughter, a sister, a nerd, a drama queen (twenty-two consecutive years, thank you very much), a reader, a professional dancer in the kitchen. But a Black woman? What does that mean, I thought. It didn't feel positive, the way I found out. If I hadn't realized this before, did that mean being a Black woman was something to be ashamed of? I remember only pausing for a moment before running back into the game, but I couldn't push it away.

I wasn't Malia, or "girl," or "her," or "you"... it was Black woman.

Only two words and less than five seconds, but at eleven, I knew that meant so much more. The ball was still in play, and who knows who was winning. We were just yelling at each other and throwing the ball like our lives depended on it. Soon enough, I was back near Chuck, who again had the ball. There was hesitation this time, but I was the closest on my team to him. I had to get the ball. I steadied myself before running up to him again and threw my hands in the air so he couldn't shoot it. He leaned to his left, so I leaned to my right. He grunted at me and shuffled to his right, and I moved with him. His face was even sweatier, and his eyes angrier. He moved to my right again, and before he could finish the movement, I smacked the ball out of his hand.

He gasped, and so did I, as the ball bounced off the court and into the hands of someone on my team. The players jogged away and headed toward the hoop, but for a moment, Chuck stood still. The glance was quick, and the word barely had a sound as he walked away from me.

"Nigger."

I couldn't feel anything. I couldn't move. The tan walls and the people in the gym became blurred, and the sound disappeared. I had never heard that word before. Not that clear. Not that defined. Not where even in the muttering, the "er" was crisp.

I don't think I truly understood what that word meant at the time, but I knew enough.

That moment gave me a theory: some words, some ideas, some situations— even if you don't fully understand what's happening— carry so much weight in this world that your body and mind can still feel the shift. I didn't know the history of that word. But I knew that it was a scornful, insulting, disrespectful term. A word that shouldn't be said.

I would have rather gotten punched.

There has never been another moment in my life where I had felt so singled out except for hearing that word. I was aware of my skin color, but had never felt so "othered." Reduced to so little, that the dirt outside the gym could've been held at a higher status. Suddenly, my name didn't matter, what I liked to do was irrelevant, and there wasn't a point to who I wanted to be. The only thing that defined me in that moment was the darkness that is my skin. It would've taken more thought for him to call me a nerd or any other arsenal in a bully's backpack. He could've given me more worth by taking time to lessen me. But a racial slur? No thought at all.

I wonder where he first heard that word. I wonder if he knew what it meant. I actively avoid gambling, but I'd put money on the idea that Chuck heard someone in his life say it in a negative way—and just followed suit. Either way, a second for him became a lifetime for me.

I don't remember class ending that day, or leaving the gym. The world had stopped spinning. Usually, after electives, we went to our homerooms for a little bit before getting picked up, but I somehow ended up at the counselor's office instead. The counselor, at the time, was a very nice Black woman. She smiled at me and asked me how my day was, and that was when I started to cry. I have no memory of what I told her, but clear as day, I recall her passing me a box of tissues and saying, "I remember the first time someone called me the 'N' word."

Was this my life now? Subjected to feel this way anytime someone decided to call me out for what was attached and I could never get off? Will someone call me that word again? Would I feel this worthless, reduced to almost nothing, again? Whatever else the counselor said to comfort me didn't, and I just wanted to go home. I went back to class and grabbed my backpack to head to the exact place where I was introduced to this new feeling. I had to sit in that same gym for a while too. I don't know if my tears ever stopped. My mom was the one who picked me and my brother up, and as soon as the car door closed, I felt ashamed. I felt I had done something wrong, somehow? Felt more alone than ever, even being back with the people who did know my name and who I am.

At the house, I finally told my mom what had happened. As I cried, she stayed silent. I couldn't tell what she was thinking, or what she wanted to do. She held me tight, told me it was all going to be okay, and we went on to the next thing. The word felt a lot bigger than the reaction, but what else was there to be done?

I had grown up.

The world had been blown apart, and now I was expected to live in it like everyone else. Whether it was too early or too late to be revealed to it, I could never tell you. Little did I know that it would take years to be exposed to Black history, Black culture, and the centuries' worth of time where people with the same skin as me were diminished to nothing. In that same building, I would go on to learn about the continual horrors my ancestors endured—lessons that slowly and calmly revealed just how little they had been valued… and how little I had been too.

In the same breath, since that day, I have gradually seen the beauty that comes with being Black. These days, my smile gets a little bigger when I bring my curls back out—oh, how beautiful is my crown of brown. I am in awe every day of all that Black human beings have created and brought into this world, and to learn about all of the movements and conversations we started or moved forward. It is an inspiration and honor every day to have descended from such power despite the odds.

My mom herself breathes her Blackness in, letting it define her with pride and strength. I aspire to do the same— to see my Blackness not as something to bear, but as something to love, to live, and to honor. I want to carry the beauty and the voice of the generations before us, breathing in their legacy and letting it shape my every step. But I can never go back to the life I lived before being called that word. In the good and in the abused, my skin cannot come off.

"Uneasy lies the head that wears a (beautiful) crown."

"They both began to giggle and then... fell into a side-splitting round of laughter, the cleansing, complete sort of laughter only a mother and daughter can share."
- Karen Kingsbury

CHAPTER THREE

Childhood

Olivia's Perspective

After first grade and moving from Rochester, New York, to Denver, Colorado, my childhood memories became a bit of a blur. At one point, my therapist told me that this was probably due to a combination of too much trauma and the constant upheaval of changing homes so frequently. I'd like to believe it's just selective memory, but either way, there are large chunks of my early years that feel like static—background noise with no clear details.

But what I do remember is that my childhood was filled with creativity.

You had to be creative when you didn't have money.

And that was the one word I felt people consistently described me as a kid—*creative*.

Not pretty, not smart, not athletic, not outgoing.

Just creative. I'll take it.

One of my favorite things to do was make anything and everything out of paper. And luckily, we had tons of it because one of my moms would bring it home from work—reams and boxes full of the stuff. We had so much that, to this day, I can still smell that old-school office paper scent, the kind that lingers in storage rooms and supply closets.

We even had those green-striped dot matrix printer paper stacks—the ones with the perforated holes on the sides that you had to tear off. You could make anything with paper and crayons—tickets, passports, library cards, paper dolls, restaurant menus, fake money. If I'd had the business savvy back then, I probably would've started a counterfeit operation and been rolling in Monopoly-style cash.

Around that time, my mom was sewing gis for my dad's karate school, so she taught me how to sew. My first project was a small handbag—then an apron. I still have them both in a box somewhere, relics of my tiny hands learning how to stitch my imagination into reality.

And then, on one of my birthdays, my dad found an old, beautiful black Singer sewing machine at a garage sale.

It's honestly the only gift I remember him actually giving me that was truly from him.

That sewing machine changed the game.

It took my love for Barbies to a whole new level because now—now I could make their clothes.

While most kids were coming up with elaborate, drama-filled Barbie soap operas, I was running a high-fashion Barbie couture house. Forget storylines; my dolls were there to *serve looks*.

It was all about dressing them, undressing them, trying on different outfits, experimenting with accessories, mixing and matching. My Barbies were my very first muses, and I was their stylist and designer.

That definitely wasn't the case with Malia.

Malia's Barbies? Oh, they had full-on identities.

First, middle, and last names. Birth dates and probably Social Security numbers.

Each doll had a background story, a family tree, a richly detailed personal history. I'm convinced that some of them even had resumes and LinkedIn profiles.

It was elaborate, to say the least.

And so, on brand for my future author of a daughter.

She quickly learned that in order to keep track of all the drama going on in Barbie Land, she had to *create spreadsheets*.

Yes, spreadsheets.

Whether on paper or electronically, she had an entire system to manage the social structure of her Barbie world.

Meanwhile, I was over here like, *what if I paired this sparkly blue top with this mini skirt?* Clearly, our brains were operating in completely different ways. But if there's one thing I know for sure, it's that both of us—Malia, the storyteller, and me, the fashion-obsessed designer—were shaped by the same thing: Barbie.

I never thought much about it until we watched the *Black Barbie* documentary together. That's when it hit us.

Barbie didn't just influence how we saw ourselves.

She influenced who we became.

For me, playing with Barbie was never about pretending to be a grown-up or playing house. It was about clothes, style, creativity, and expression—which, in many ways, set the foundation for my love of branding, design, and entrepreneurship.

For Malia, it was storytelling, world-building, and character development—which would later lead her to become an author before she even graduated high school.

Barbie was never just a doll.

She was the beginning of something. Even if we didn't realize it at the time. Back then, I didn't like my name.

It was different. Weird.

No one else was named Olivia. There were no O initial keychains, no personalized magnets, no coffee mugs with my name on them at the store. Nothing.

Olivia was a name that stood out.

And at six years old, I *did not* want to stand out.

I wanted to belong.

I was certain that when I grew up, I would change my name to something more common. Something normal.

Like Jennifer, perhaps.

Jennifer was everywhere. There were always at least *two* in my class, maybe even three. And they all seemed to have this built-in sisterhood—instant best friends bonded by their shared, beautifully ordinary name.

Meanwhile, there I was... *Olivia*.

The only one.

It felt unfair.

Ironically, I adore my name now and get compliments on it all the time—people say it sounds like a movie star or a superhero.

If only my younger self knew.

The name Olivia has been in the top three of popular girl names for years now.

It seems like I can't go anywhere without hearing a mom calling out, "Olivia, put that down!" or "Olivia, come here!"

It took some getting used to—not turning around every time I heard it in public, feeling personally called out by a stranger disciplining their child.

A few years ago, I was having dinner at a popular pasta place in Boulder. It was one of my favorite spots during college—the *same* place where I ordered my first drink after turning 21. Though, to this day, I still have no idea how I ever afforded it back then.

When I ordered a glass of wine, the young college student waiting on my table asked to check my ID. I handed it over, feeling slightly flattered by the request.

She stared at my license longer than normal, and I assumed it was because she couldn't find my birth year. After all, 1979 must seem ancient—probably only recognizable as a PIN or a password.

But then she looked up at me, wide-eyed, and said, "My name's also Olivia. And we have the same birthday."

I was stunned.

Giddy, even.

TWIN! I wanted to scream. I had waited my whole life for this moment. Where had she been all my life? A fellow Olivia. A birthday twin! I could barely contain myself.

The lonely first grader in me wanted to leap out of her seat, hug this girl tight, and immediately ask for her phone number or Instagram.

But instead, I kept it together, smiled, and said, "That's so cool."

Inside, though?

Inside, I was still that little girl longing for connection—for someone to twin with, to share the experience of having my name.

But Jennifer… Jennifer was different.

Jennifer was beautiful—at least according to my six-year-old standard of beauty. Not too tall, not too skinny—just right. I imagined that she would grow up to look just like Barbie.

Perfect.

She had the most brilliant blue eyes—the kind of blue that only existed in clear summer skies and Crayola 64-pack markers.

And her hair—oh, her hair.

It was long, straight, golden blonde—the kind that flowed when she moved, like something out of a television commercial.

Her hair had motion—it swayed with the lightest breeze, like a Disney princess brought to life.

My hair? My hair didn't move. It stayed stuck in place. Stiff. Unshakable.

My mom would call the back of my hair, near the nape of my neck, a "dirty kitchen."

As a child, I internalized that—dirty like my skin, I thought. My hair was difficult, almost unruly, like it had its own mind, its own agenda. And it wasn't the kind of hair that could be free. It had to be tamed, controlled, punished into submission. I cried whenever my mom braided my hair into cornrows—not just because of the relentless tugging and pulling, but because it made me look even more different.

It cemented the reality that my hair would never move like Jennifer's, never float in the wind, never glisten under the fluorescent lights of my first-grade classroom.

I wanted it to be free. To move like Barbie's. To some have motion.

I begged my mom to let me wear it out, and one day—one glorious day—she finally agreed.

It was Halloween, 1986.

My costume? A punk rocker. My hair? Not just out, but spray-painted orange and purple. I wore a short black skirt (with jeans underneath, of course—modesty was still enforced), a bright, colorful top slung off one shoulder, gold chains, and makeup. For a few hours, I felt different. Lighter. My hair was wild and free, and for the briefest moment, I felt a little bit like Jennifer. I didn't have her golden hair or her sky-blue eyes, but for the first time, I didn't feel the weight of my difference—so much. But as the night ended, reality crept back in.

The braids had to return.

My hair went back into its familiar confinement.

Back to jail you go, I thought bitterly, beginning what would become a lifelong, complicated relationship with my hair—one that would define me, deceive me, and divide me from who I thought I was supposed to be.

Because in reality?

I was ridiculously skinny, awkward, with an overbite that I utterly loathe to this day (why was I not one of the lucky kids who got braces?).

I was completely obsessed with Michael Jackson—despite the plastic surgeries that started in the early '90s.

Mark Wahlberg was still Marky Mark, and the number one song was "I Wanna Sex You Up" by Color Me Badd.

Beauty and the Beast and *Hook* were the *greatest* movies of all time.

And I had *big* dreams.

I was going to be a fashion designer—spending hours upon hours sketching, sewing, and crocheting clothes for my Barbie dolls.

I drew new designs weekly and mailed them to Mattel through the Barbie Fan Club mailing address.

I made sure to include a return address so they could properly thank me for my contributions to Barbie fashion.

I'm still waiting for the phone to ring.

Or, at the very least, a few dollars in royalties for the gowns that mysteriously hit the shelves and looked suspiciously similar to mine.

It didn't really click until Malia and I watched the Black Barbie documentary on Netflix—decades later, sitting side by side, both of us suddenly seeing the role Barbie had played in shaping us.

Barbie, from both of our childhoods, had not just defined our early perceptions of beauty and self-worth—she had influenced our careers.

Looking back, it was so obvious. I had spent my childhood sketching designs, selling Barbie clothes, and forcing my little sister to model for my living room fashion shows (against her will, of course).

Malia, on the other hand, built worlds.

Her Barbies had full government names, backstories, birthdates, and probably Social Security numbers. They had relationships, conflicts, drama. She had to create spreadsheets just to track the elaborate storylines she was spinning. Of course, she became a writer before she even entered high school. Of course, she dedicated herself to storytelling, bringing to life characters just as complex as the ones who lived in her childhood bedroom.

Barbie had prepared her for this.

And she had prepared me, too.

Because long before I ever knew what I wanted to do, I was already becoming it. It wasn't just Barbie, though. Creativity was woven into the fabric of my childhood, not just through play, but through necessity. We didn't have a lot, so we made a lot.

Paper was transformed into passports for made-up vacations, library cards for an imaginary book collection, tickets for pretend concerts starring Whitney Houston (me) and Janet Jackson (also me).

I created out of need, and that need turned into love.

Love for art. Love for self-expression. Love for building something out of nothing.

And now I realize—this wasn't just play. This was training.

Training to be an entrepreneur.

Training to be a creator. Training to be the kind of person who *sees* the world differently—not as it is, but as it *could be*.

And that mindset? That spark?
It followed me into adulthood.

It shaped the way I approached every new challenge, every career path, every bold idea I had no business pursuing but did anyway.

Creativity made me fearless.
Creativity saved me.

Because before I had a plan, before I had a career, before I had any real sense of direction, I had this.

I had my paper and crayons. I had my Barbies and my sketches. I had my mom's sewing skills and my dad's garage sale Singer. I had a million ideas and no one telling me they weren't possible.

And maybe, just maybe, that was enough to carry me forward.

To this moment.

To the life that awaited me.

To the career I hadn't yet imagined but was already being built—one sketch, one stitch, one dream at a time.

Malia's Perspective

My earliest memories of play involved truly being a princess. I wasn't just pretending—I lived it. I wore princess dresses all the time, flowing gowns that made me feel like royalty. My closet overflowed with glitter, tulle, and satin, and I took every opportunity to transform into a fairytale vision. Tea parties were a regular event, carefully arranged with stuffed animals and dolls as my royal guests. The delicate clinking of plastic tea cups set the scene as I sipped imaginary tea and practiced my most graceful curtsy.

But above all, I danced. I twirled, twirled, and twirled some more, spinning through my childhood with a sense of freedom that only dance could bring. Dancing wasn't just an activity—it was a staple of my childhood, a core part of who I was. I poured everything into each movement, into every step, leap, and turn. Recital after recital, I knew the songs by heart, feeling the rhythm pulse through me. More often than not, I was placed front and center, a position I didn't take lightly. It wasn't about being seen—it was about expressing something bigger than words could capture.

From ballet slippers to tap shoes, I embraced the stage, adorned in gorgeous gems and sparkling costumes that made me feel even more like a princess. But the stage was never the only place I danced. The moment the music started—whether in the studio, the car, or at home—I couldn't help but move. I filled every room with choreography of my own making, perfecting routines that only I knew. Each step, each spin was a story, a performance that carried my emotions and imagination to new heights.

One performance, in particular, has gone down in family history. I danced so hard, so passionately, that my teal bow flew off in the middle of the routine. But I didn't stop. I kept going, just like our dance teacher taught us, completely immersed in the music and the moment. That memory—that fearless devotion to my craft—still stands as one of the purest reflections of how deeply I pour myself into the things I love. Dancing wasn't just about movement; it was about storytelling, about creating a world where I could be anyone, express anything, and let my heart lead the way.

The twirls, the tiaras, the gowns—I loved stepping into a role, letting movement and performance tell my stories. Even when I wasn't on a stage, I was still creating. My world was full of characters and dreams, and no one embodied that more than Barbie. She wasn't just a doll; she was a blank canvas, ready for whatever story I wanted to tell. And just like I twirled and danced as a princess, I crafted entire lives for my Barbies.

I lost my mind over my first Barbie doll, and as my collection grew—including the one and only Ken—I played with them constantly. My Barbies lived my life alongside me: they attended school assemblies, went to church (literally, I brought them to church), and even re-enacted cafeteria drama. On weekends, they were just as busy as I was.

When I looked at my Barbies, I didn't just see plastic and bright pink lipstick, I saw a world. Each Barbie had a name, a personality, a unique style. Were they popular or bookish? The life of the party or a wallflower? Once that was decided, the show began. I sketched out their lives in notebooks, deciding where they lived, who their families were, and what roles they played. Sometimes, they were high schoolers at real schools in my area. Other times, they were college students at CU Boulder or, reluctantly, at Colorado State. Some became doctors, teachers, lawyers, or journalists. My stories spanned weeks, sometimes months, before I moved on to the next adventure.

Romance was always at the heart of my Barbie stories. For at least a week, Tess, Katie, Harper, and Ally ruled Grandview University. Three were blonde with blue eyes, one had black hair and brown eyes, and they effortlessly commanded attention. They lived in the best house—five shelves high—with the iconic Barbie convertible parked outside. But everything changed when Ken arrived. He had golden hair, piercing blue eyes, and a charm that captivated everyone. Soon, Tess became his leading lady, and together, they were the talk of the campus.

In every adventure, Ken always chose someone. Whether it was Tess, Carol, or Kayley, romance dictated the storyline. As I got older, one Ken wasn't enough. I used my babysitting money to buy more Kens, ensuring every girl had a love story of her own. With fourteen new Kens, my Barbie world expanded, but love remained the centerpiece. I poured into these stories because, in reality, romance always seemed just out of reach for me. I was never the girl who got asked out, never had a secret admirer, never got a "prom-posal". So, my Barbies lived out my dreams—Maria had a secret admirer, Kimberly got an elaborate "prom-posal", and Caroline adored Valentine's Day. If I couldn't experience love, at least my Barbies could.

Years later, Greta Gerwig's *Barbie* movie hit, and I found myself laughing, crying, and confronting the expectations I had unknowingly embraced. Then, my mom and I watched Netflix's *Black Barbie* documentary, and everything clicked.

That, of all stories, brought me back to Tess and Ken—the couple who ruled Grandview University—the day Ken saw Jasmine. With her long black hair, warm brown eyes, and radiant smile, Jasmine was different. Intrigued, Ken sought her out, and soon, they were walking hand-in-hand across campus. The scandal! The betrayal!

Looking back, I realized something unsettling. Tess was white, while Jasmine was one of my two Black Barbies. In all my stories, somehow, my Black Barbies were never the stars. They were always the side characters—the best friends or, worse, the *other woman*. I had at least one Barbie who looked like me, yet I never chose her. Instead, I favored my white Barbies—the ones I saw as prettier, with "better" hair, the ones Ken would pick in real life. And the painful truth? I had full control over these stories. I named them, I shaped their lives, and still, I pushed the Black Barbies to the background. Since I was a little girl, I overlooked my beauty, my value, and what I bring to the table.

Shonda Rhimes put it perfectly in the documentary: *"If you've gone your whole life and never seen anything made in your own image, there is damage done."* Even though Black Barbies existed when I was growing up, they weren't central in movies or TV shows. At school, the Black girl was always the best friend, never the main character. I couldn't accept what I looked like because it wasn't "pretty" or "normal." The white doll—the white Barbie—was prettier, and she was the "it" girl at school.

Without realizing it, I internalized this hierarchy, casting myself as a background character in my own imagination. Black girls were on the bench of all the headlines, or worse, cast aside. Whether I knew it or not, that's what I felt like in the real world.

Watching the documentary with my mom was bittersweet. There was pride, of course—Mattel was finally acknowledging Black girls by creating Black Barbies. It made me feel seen, loved, beautiful. But it also made me sad. It took *twenty-one years* for a Black doll to be called "Barbie." Even then, she arrived so late that girls like me still saw the original Barbie as the standard of beauty. Today, Black women are still the best friends in dolls, movies, and shows—never the main characters. Progress is important, but it doesn't erase what was lost. It should've never taken that long to recognize little Black girls too. And even with Barbie's advancements, I can't shake the feeling of being second. Is there a world, even an imaginary one, where Black women come first?

I guess my fairy tales at home couldn't be completely imaginary.

That realization was heartbreaking. Since I was a little girl, I had overlooked my own beauty, my value, and my worth. My Barbies helped me dream, escape, and discover my love for storytelling—but they also revealed something deeper. Even in my own world of make-believe, the stories I told with my Barbies weren't just fantasy—they reflected what I saw and felt in real life. If I had unknowingly placed myself in the background of my own stories, where else had I done the same?

Barbie gave me endless possibilities, but sometimes, I wanted to live out the stories myself. My imagination didn't just live in the plastic world of dolls; it spilled into the spaces around me. From the moment I could create my own stories and play my own games, I was drawn to those that resembled real life. While other kids might have dreamed up far-off lands filled with fairies, dragons, and castles in the sky, my imagination stayed a little closer to home. The games I played weren't about escaping into fantasy but about building a world I could understand—one that made sense to me.

One of my favorite games to play was school. Every year before the first day, my brother and I would grab our brand-new backpacks, feeling the excitement of the fresh start that came with each school year. We didn't wait for the actual bus to pick us up—we had one of our own. My mom's closet transformed into our bus, the dark, enclosed space making it feel like we were really on the way to something new and important. We sat in our imaginary (tight) seats, bouncing slightly as if feeling the bumps in the road, chattering about the "school day" ahead. Once we arrived at our destination, we stepped out, ready to learn, teach, or just pretend that we were living the lives of students who had it all figured out.

At my grandma's house, my world expanded even further. My mini couch wasn't just a couch—it was my bed, a symbol of stability and routine. Every night, I tucked my child (who happened to be my brother) into bed, making sure he was comfortable before turning in myself. I played the role of the caring, responsible mother, the one who made sure everything was just as it should be. I was in charge—making the rules, providing comfort, and creating the kind of home life that felt steady and whole.

Even with my friends, the theme of real life remained. If I got to pick the game, we wouldn't be warriors on an epic quest or witches casting spells—we were a family going to school, navigating the everyday joys and struggles of life. Sometimes, our games even stretched as far as a wedding, where two of us would get married in a ceremony we designed ourselves. I'm pretty sure I'm in a marriage to at least two different girls from the middle school playground. Even then, the story stayed rooted in reality, reflecting the things we saw and the relationships we longed to understand.

Looking back, I find it fascinating how my young mind instinctively shaped stories that mirrored life as I wished it to be. While I lived in a world where some things felt uncertain—where home didn't always look the same and life sometimes shifted without warning—I built a world where I had control. In my games, I decided how things played out. If we got on the bus in one room, I knew exactly where it would take us. If I was a mother, I knew my child was safe. If we were a family, I knew we would stay together. The unpredictability of real life faded away in my carefully structured stories. It's what I needed, I supposed, to feel happy and safe.

At home, it was just my mom, my brother, and me. I was a child, not the mother I pretended to be. And sometimes, the bus we rode in my game meant something more: we really did move from one room to another, from one home to another. Sometimes we were with my dad, and sometimes we weren't. Things changed in real life in ways I couldn't understand or control—in ways I didn't like. But in my imaginary world, nothing got flipped on its head unless I chose for it to. I held the reins, deciding how the day would go, what my family would look like, and how our lives would unfold. If I couldn't control what my life would look like, at least I could control my life in my own little world.

In many ways, the games I played were just as imaginative as fairy tales and mythical adventures, but they carried a different kind of magic. Instead of escaping to a place filled with unicorns and enchanted forests, I created a space where life made sense, where love was steady, and where home was always home. I felt safe there, in those games. My stories weren't about slaying dragons or saving kingdoms—they were about finding security, writing a reality where I knew the ending, and making sense of a world that, at times, felt just out of my grasp.

I built entire worlds in my games, ones where I had control, where I got to decide how the story unfolded. I played out those stories because the real world wasn't always as predictable. Outside of my amazing dolls, and my games, I did have friendships that filled my days with immense joy. For the most part, I can remember all the friends I've had throughout school and life, and they all meant so much to me. There were two girls I went to elementary school with; they were my best friends. We hung out whenever we could—class, recess—and when planning sleepovers, they were the first two I invited. We played a ton of pretend, creating whole worlds from the cracks in the sidewalk and the corners of the playground. We giggled—a lot. We could poke fun at each other and laugh at the things we did, until one day, it wasn't funny.

It was second grade, maybe third. We were sitting in the gym-turned-cafeteria with our lunches. I always got a hot lunch that came with a milk carton, and I got chocolate milk every time. We were laughing about who knows what, and for my whole life, my laughter has always been loud, using my entire body. I laughed and laughed and laughed—until I knocked my milk carton over. The chocolate spilled across the table and started to drip onto the gym floor. All three of us started laughing all over again, but something was different. The girls were looking at me—more than before. Their eyes were locked onto mine, their fingers pointing, their laughter stretching too long.

It wasn't a giggle or even laughter. It was like they were laughing at me. I laughed for a moment, but soon, I stopped.

"Malia is always spilling her milk!"

No. No, I don't.

The milk dripped onto my uniform, and my heart started to beat faster. It wasn't funny—not the way they were looking at me. If I wasn't laughing with them, why were they still going? I suddenly felt small, my cheeks burning as I hurried to clean up the mess. We always laughed together, but how often was it at me? How many times had I been the joke without realizing it?

That was the first time they laughed at me. They did it again at kickball.

Music would play during P.E., and on kickball days, when it was your team's turn to kick, you had to wait in line. I found that boring, so I would dance beside my spot—twirl, twist, kick, and flare. Dancing like no one was watching. But suddenly, someone was giggling.

I opened my eyes, and my uniform skirt slowed as I saw my friends across the gym, laughing at me. What was so funny? They were pointing at me while they twirled their pretend skirts and threw themselves through the air in exaggerated, mocking movements. My smile faltered, and I stepped back in line.

Oh. It was me. I'm the joke.

But they're my friends. Friends don't do that, right?

Around that time, one of those girls even told me I was annoying, and my smile would shrink even more. I believed friendship meant being chosen, but I guess it was only if I wasn't too much—too weird, too happy, too me.

Every game, every character, every scene I dreamed up left fingerprints on who I was becoming. As a princess, I spun across the living room, lost in glitter and possibility. With Barbies, I built cities, families, drama, and peace—whole worlds I could control. School and family games weren't just pretend; they were practice. They gave order to the chaos. And in friendship, I learned that laughter could be a bridge—or a wall. Being picked didn't always mean being seen.

I didn't know it then, but I was always searching—for reflection, for belonging, for a story where I got to be the main character. Those early games weren't just for fun. They were how I made sense of things I didn't yet have words for. And even now, the pieces remain. My love for storytelling became writing, my passion for performance shaped how I express myself, and my need to create safe spaces influenced how I navigate relationships.

Now, I embrace my own story—one where I'm not a side character but the protagonist, fully seen and fully valued. Little me—I'm sorry you thought you had to sit on the side of your own story. But you don't have to anymore.

"When someone asks you where you come from, the answer is your mother."
- Anna Quindlen

CHAPTER FOUR

Career

Olivia's Perspective

Since my little stint in New York City right after graduation, my nothing-but-linear career has taken quite a few tosses and turns—some dizzying, some divine. I've spent a good amount of time as an advertising executive and branding consultant, working on some of the biggest brands in the world and some of the smallest local initiatives. But let's be real, my career didn't start in a sleek conference room or through some flashy LinkedIn connection.

It started way back when with a box of fabric scraps and a vision.

My very first business was born in childhood after the "warm up" of sewing Barbie clothes—I graduated to making and selling clothes for stuffed animals. Yes, you read that right. I ran this enterprise mostly through local craft stores and custom orders, back when the "Interwebs" were still a glimmer in Al Gore's eye.

The business model?

Simple genius: customize and dress your own stuffed animal and build a personalized gift basket around it. And yes, I wrote my first business plan around this concept. That plan went on to take first place at state in DECA, the high school business and marketing club that would go on to shape my passion for marketing.

I used the *exact same* plan—printed, bound, and sprinkled with hope—in an entrepreneurship class in college. Does this concept sound familiar? Well, in true "God has jokes" fashion, Maxine Clark launched Build-A-Bear Workshop later that same year. All that did was confirm what I already knew: the idea was solid! And I was clearly ahead of my time. A future millionaire—missed it by that much.

But God, in all His intentionality, had other plans.

From there, the ventures just kept coming. Graphic design. Web design. A stationery company I ran on the side to make extra cash. I launched a children's clothing line on *The Ellen DeGeneres Show*. I started a PR and marketing collective made up of Colorado-based mom and baby companies. Ran my own branding and marketing firm. Launched a faith-based journal company. Designed a T-shirt upcycling fanny pack line.

I know—I need a nap just reading that list.

If you're not an entrepreneur yourself, you might look at all that and think, "Wow, she's a little all over the place." And to that I say—

yes. Yes, I am. But it's a purposeful kind of chaos. What ties it all together is creativity and storytelling. Every project, every pivot, has been rooted in identity, voice, branding and belonging. I wasn't flailing; I was evolving. Shifting. Searching for fulfillment in roles that could house the fullness of who I truly am.

And that's the thing about belonging—it changes shape as we do.

These days, I find myself speaking more and more on the topic of belonging, authenticity, and what it means to show up in the spaces where we work, learn, play, and live—especially when you're "the only one."

The only woman.

The only mom.

The only Black woman.

The only Gen-Xer in a room full of TikTokers.

We've all heard the rally cries: "Bring your whole self to work!" "Be your authentic self!" They sound empowering—until you realize that these calls are often directed at the people least safe to do so. These phrases become band-aids for a deeper wound. Because let's be honest, I don't even bring my full authentic self to family gatherings. Finding a space that truly embraces all of you, without asking you to shrink or code-switch, is hard.

It's exhausting trying to stand out and belong at the same time.

The wise Brene Brown says it best:

> *"Stop walking through the world looking for confirmation that you don't belong. You will always find it because you've made that your mission... True belonging and self-worth are not goods; we don't negotiate their value with the world. The truth about who we are lives in our hearts. Our call to courage is to protect our wild heart against constant evaluation, especially our own."*

I didn't understand this in my twenties or even my thirties. I spent so many years trying to decode spaces that weren't built with me in mind—trying to read the room, play the part, fit the mold. But I've learned that if I change myself just to fit in with you, then I no longer belong to me.

Belonging isn't just about saying, "You're welcome here." It's about the space saying, "We wouldn't be complete without you here." Not just *you're included*—but *you're essential.*

And that realization changes everything.

For so many of us—especially women, especially women of color—it's difficult to find careers, industries, or companies where we can stop performing. Where we can drop the mask, lose the code-switching (or at least reduce it), and show up fully without the emotional toll. Sometimes, we can't even envision what that might look like—because we've never seen it modeled.

I didn't know exactly what I wanted to be when I grew up in part because I never saw it in existence. I just knew I wanted to do something big. Something with impact. Something so meaningful that people would remember my name.

Go back and listen to the theme song from *Fame*, the show that premiered in 1982.

"Baby, remember my name!"

This was Irene Cara's ultimate declaration. It wasn't about fame for the sake of attention. It was about leaving a legacy. Making your mark. Creating something that lasts beyond you.

That's always been my driving force—impact and legacy.

As a kid, I rotated through a range of ambitious career goals: fashion designer, singer, ballerina, cheerleader, pediatrician. That last one was before my eyes glazed over in first biology class and before my heart was swept away by marketing. But no matter the title, I always had two constants: I wanted to *create*, and I wanted to *lead*. Whether I was crafting clothes, building brands, or writing stories, I was always building something.

And then there was Malia.

Malia, who had spreadsheets tracking the relationships of her Barbies. Malia, who could tell you the full backstory of a doll she'd just unboxed. Malia, who gave her dolls first, last and middle names, childhood traumas, love interests, and five-year career goals. She was out here building HR files for her Barbies while I was just sewing dresses for them hoping Mattel would cut me a little check.

Watching her play was like watching a tiny CEO or a mini executive creative director in action. She wasn't just imagining—she was building—a full-fledged Barbie storytelling empire. And that was when it clicked for me: We'd both been shaping our futures long before we knew what they would look like.

It was only later that I realized—Malia and I were *already* shaping our futures even as little girls.

She would go on to become a writer, effortlessly crafting complex stories and characters. And me? I was unknowingly preparing myself for a life of storytelling too—not through fiction, but through branding, marketing, and the power of sharing and shaping narratives.

The signs had always been there.

I tell Malia's story often when I speak to audiences—actually, let's be honest, I *always* talk about her when I speak. I use her as an illustration of what it means to move through the world with confidence in your identity, with ownership of your story. She's the example of our younger selves that so many of us have lost along the way.

This past summer, we hit the road together—driving from Denver to Salida to Vail and back again. The goal? To keynote two different conferences in two different towns, reaching over 500 women in just forty-eight hours.

And we did it. Together.

The first room was filled with women business owners. The second, women attorneys. Both groups came hungry for authenticity—for ways to share their stories without shrinking themselves. Malia came ready. She was my assistant, timekeeper, photographer, hype woman, and spiritual mirror all in one. We were pure synergy.

By the time the tenth woman came up to us to say, "You two have something special. You should do something together," we paused. We listened.

And then lightning struck our brains!

We knew exactly what we had to do—find a place to sit down, lock in, pop some Prosecco (actually pop Prosecco *then* lock in), take out some paper, and begin mapping out what would become *Through Her Eyes,* born in that divine moment of connection. The energy was like nothing I had felt before—both of our creative minds firing and synching at the same time. God gave us the entire vision right there, and we had one year to execute it.

Right there, in the stillness between conference sessions and hotel room debriefs, God gave us the idea for this book. We scribbled down our thoughts, called it "Operation Whistledown" (we had just finished watching season 3 of Bridgerton on Netflix) and said yes to the assignment. It felt like the beginning of something bigger than either one of us.

And, as it always seems to go, that weekend sparked a chain reaction: more keynote invitations, more speaking engagements, a mother/daughter podcast, and a confirmation that this—*this*—is where I'm meant to be in this season.

Looking back now, I know I was never built for a "normal" career. I was never going to land a safe job, climb a tidy corporate ladder, and retire with a gold watch. I wasn't built for boxes. I was built for reinvention.

For creation.
For disruption.

In college, I thought advertising would be my thing. I pictured myself in a sleek Manhattan office, brainstorming Super Bowl commercials and sipping lattes with strategy teams. And for a while, that dream felt real. God opened doors—from Boulder to New York and back again—that allowed me to cut my. teeth on everything from brand positioning to market research to ad campaigns about almonds, potato chips and diaper wipes. It wasn't always glamorous, but it gave me the foundation I needed.

And yet, even then, I knew I wasn't meant to stay in one lane.

Over the years, my career has taken shapes I never expected. There have been victories and heartbreaks. There were times when I felt like I was just about there... only to realize I needed to pivot again. And there were moments I sat in my car or on my bathroom floor, asking, "Did I just make the worst mistake of my life?"

What I've learned?

The best careers aren't built on perfect plans. They're shaped by life. By experience.

By risk.
By failure and faith.
By trusting that even your detours are part of the map.

I used to think a "calling" meant finally arriving in the one God-given place where you're supposed to be. Now I see that a calling is more like a God-given thread—one that weaves through every job, every season, every reinvention.

Mine? That thread has always been creating something that speaks, that tells a story. Something that shapes. Something that leaves a mark.

Whether I'm branding a startup, mentoring a woman-owned business, launching a line of fanny packs (yes, that happened), sharing the importance of college and the resilient stories students, or co-authoring a book with my daughter—I'm storytelling and building.

When it comes to career, stop looking for the perfect path. Just walk. Take the next step. Try the thing. Learn as you go. Then when you look back, look for the threads.

Because your career isn't something you find.

It's something you create.

Malia's Perspective

I tell people that I've been a reader for as long as I can remember, and if you know me, you know that I used to inhale books without blinking. But the more I think about it, there was a moment when I went from someone who read to a reader. Every reader, I feel, has one.

I was roughly in third grade, and at that point, I knew how to read and could read well, but I wasn't obsessed with reading. I didn't own a lot of books and only read a book from time to time. One day, my dad suggested that he and I start a book club, just the two of us. My dad is a math teacher, so not the biggest reader, but I thought it would be fun to try something new and spend some time with him. He had found a book he thought I'd like, and he already had the first book for both of us. It was the first book in *The Series of Unfortunate Events* series, and little did I know that it was also the first page in my reading journey. The story was a slow burn, but I quickly fell in love with the book and finished it in no time. So quickly, in fact, that my dad already couldn't keep up. The book club ended almost as quickly as it had started, but he encouraged me to continue the series. In total, the series has thirteen books, and while I didn't finish the entire series when I first started, it led me to loads of other books I wanted to read. I started checking out multiple books at the library—books that were in a fourth- and fifth-grade reading level. By the time I reached fourth grade, I had one in my backpack at all times. I was reading multiple books at once (four or five at the same time, I might add), and my mom and teacher had to stage an impromptu intervention to get me to stop.

Third grade was also a pivotal year because it was the start of my writing journey. Parts of this memory are fuzzy, but in my Language Arts class, we read a story. Once we were done, our teacher asked us a question: If we could write one more page to this story and change the ending, what would we write? We were sent home with this homework assignment, and at first, I had no idea what I wanted to write. But after sitting with it and thinking, suddenly, my ideas burst through like a dam breaking. The names on a page evolved into people—these characters in my mind. The story was alive, and I wanted to add more and more to my extension of this world. I turned in the one-pager as requested, but I remember writing five to ten more pages. Along with those were other pages with notes on my new story—diagrams of the plot and the way all the characters were connected. I had written down all of their professions, their likes and dislikes, and what they wanted to do next in life. I couldn't put any of it down.

Like I mentioned with my Barbies, I carried this storytelling trait into my daily play. Even though my full-blown stories weren't written down, everything about each story was. Just like in third grade, I had everything written down about each of my Barbies, and I made new pages with each new tale—who lived in which houses, who went to which school, who was dating Ken at the time, and who picked up whom in the convertible. And with everything I wrote down, there were even more details swirling around in my head.

After a while, my Barbie playing and my storytelling faded, and I didn't pick it up again until I was in seventh grade. I still loved to read, and I was starting to watch some of my favorite fantasy and mystery TV shows, so I'm assuming that's where my first creative idea was born.

At my charter school, all of the students were assigned a number when they started attending. This number was given to parents, guardians, and grandparents, and they put it on a sticker on their car. This was the building block of the school's pickup system. All of the parents would pull up to the school, and there was a strip of concrete that looped around it. As the parents slowly drove around, the students sat in the gym with their grade, waiting for their number to be called. The teachers outside would read all the numbers in the next section of cars and radio those numbers to the gym. By the time I got to seventh grade, I had already done the carpool system for years, so my number was memorized, and I usually thought about a million other things while waiting.

One day, I was sitting against the gym wall, letting my thoughts drift as usual. I watched groups of students exit the school and walk to the strip of concrete, where the playground also was. I closed my eyes and thought about the swings out there and how kids would swing back and forth, back and forth. I thought about it and, randomly, I wondered... What if the kids disappeared? Off the swings? I sat up in shock, slightly grinning at my thought. I went home, and without thinking, I started to write. All the ideas rushed to my brain, flowed through my fingers, and onto the computer. I had no idea where I was going or what I was doing, but I was excited about it.

When I started to create my characters, I didn't really know who was going to star in my story. It could've been anyone, really. But if I was going to write about swings that sat outside my school, why not write about the people who go to the school? A weight was lifted off my shoulders when my characters lined themselves up in the hallway, and besides, who could write my friends better than me? With my friends and classmates added, naturally, I became the main character—Melissa Logan. I couldn't forget about my siblings, my dad (a.k.a. the math teacher), my stepmom, and—though I will never remember why—the ultimate villain was attached to this person. Mom, I am so sorry you were the villain. I swear I don't remember why. Anyway, the characters had their marks, the stage was set, and my fingers flew across the keyboard.

Around the same time, one of my friends was entering a writing contest, and I wanted to join her. The maximum word count was five thousand. I wrote every chance I had, and when I was done fleshing out an idea, another came knocking. The five-thousand-word limit was blown out of the water, and I had to cut it down before I could submit it. I remember the anticipation, the fear, the adrenaline right before I clicked the button. Texting my friend at the same time, we both pressed submit together. It was five minutes of being on top of the world, followed by devastation. The next screen was an award for participation; everyone was a winner. Like, come on, what was the point of a contest if everyone got an award? Looking back, though, I guess there was a purpose, because that ending also gave me a lightbulb moment. What else was next except to continue the story? The spring was back like it had never left, and I wrote and wrote until I had nearly forty thousand words and a mountain of notes.

It was an out-of-body experience, realizing that I had pretty much written a book. At just thirteen years old. Even today, people ask me how I did it, and my response is always that I just did it. I had a whole world in my head, and I breathed it onto paper. It was pure joy—building a world, a story—and I was the puppet master. Both the director and the recorder, watching my characters and writing what happened. When I finished what is now called *The Death Call*, no one knew I had written it, not even my mom. It was my little secret hobby. But once I finished it, the fun was over, and I wanted more. So, naturally, I started writing the sequel. The ideas were bigger and flowed faster, and I couldn't stop.

With my little secret, I never imagined it could be more. It was just me and the barely functioning computer in the basement. I guess I thought I would write forever and simply keep the files. It was the journey, the characters, and me, all in our little corner. By the time my fourteenth birthday rolled around, I was over halfway done writing the sequel, and that was when the book became bigger than just my basement.

It was the end of January, and I had just finished a basketball game. I don't remember the score—I just remember having fun and then losing. It was a common occurrence during my seventh-grade year, but you got used to it. Afterward, my mom and grandma took us out to dinner to celebrate my birthday. Our birthday, rather. After dinner, dessert, and laughs, my mom pulled out a present for me. It looked like a book, which was no surprise to me. Another one! I ripped open the wrapping paper, and I saw the words *The Death Call* staring back at me. The title was in purple, dripping letters, with a desk behind it. Underneath the desk was the name M.J. Logan, and it took me a moment to recognize my own last name. Were M and J my initials? I couldn't process what it was or how it had come to be. That was my book—but I was holding it? I do this thing where if I'm nervous, I smile, so my confused smile was what I did when I looked up at my mom. She smiled back at me, and I grinned. She is the coolest person I know.

"How did you do this?" I asked.

"I took your document and printed out your book," she explained as I turned the book in my hands. I couldn't stop smiling at the idea of holding my own book, my words inside. My photo was on the back, and my world was waiting for me to explore! Happiness bubbled up inside me as I anxiously waited to put my work on the same shelf as my *Harry Potter* and *Divergent* books. We went home, and all I could think about was racing to my room, but thankfully, my mom wasn't done showing me what was possible.

"We can self-publish your book and sell them," she said with a smile, showing me her computer. My mom opened a door that night, one I didn't even know existed. It had never occurred to me that the joy I found in writing could be shared with others. I never realized that other people—kids—could read my work. Maybe, just maybe, they could even enjoy what I had to say.

Looking back, I found my career because of my mom. She showed me that I could do something with what I loved. She helped me redesign the cover, edit the book, self-publish my first book and the ones that followed, and even taught me how to buy my own books. She shared everything she had learned in her career and became the best wing woman I could ask for. Through her, I learned how to market my books and how to invest money to make it back. She connected me with different marketplaces to sell my books, organizations that could help my business grow, and even built my original website. I may have written the books, but she was—and still is—the backbone of *The Death Call*. I wouldn't have been able to do any of it without her. She showed me that I could make money doing what I love. Past that, and more importantly, the books I created allowed me to visit classrooms and students, supporting their writing and encouraging them to follow their dreams. Every kid that I interacted with, and who read my book, I got to have an impact on.

Since my *Death Call* era, I have finished high school, and thanks to this discovery and writing journey, my goal became to study creative writing in college. I love the books I self-published, but I wrote them with no experience and no formal lessons in creative writing. I didn't know how to piece words together like my favorite authors. I wanted to learn, and after searching, I found a scholarship from Angie Thomas, the author of *The Hate U Give*. In a leap of faith, I applied to Belhaven University, received the scholarship, and have since been able to grow in my craft.

Once a student reaches their final year in the creative writing program, they must complete and submit what is known as a Capstone project. This is an extensive piece of writing, divided into two main components. The first is a research paper focused on aesthetics—the philosophical study of beauty and artistic expression—which includes an analysis of our own writing within the aesthetic framework. The second, equally significant portion, is a creative piece. This could take the form of poetry, short fiction, nonfiction, or a longer fiction piece—whatever genre best represents the student's strengths and passions. The purpose of this project is to serve as the culmination of our four years in the program, showcasing everything we have learned. Both the research and creative pieces must be tied together by a common theme, creating a cohesive and meaningful study of a singular idea. Even in a marvelous story, it had to land somewhere.

We are introduced to this project as freshmen, and throughout our time in the program, it lingers in the back of our minds as an eventual challenge we will have to face. Yet, as I approached my senior year, I struggled with what direction to take. I loved writing fiction, particularly fantasy, but how could I conduct research on a world that only existed in my head? This question followed me through junior year and into the summer before my senior year, when the reality of the project loomed closer. I still had no idea what to do.

Seeking both a distraction and joy, I joined my mom in the mountains, where she was scheduled to speak at two different conferences. The first was a women's entrepreneurship conference in Salida, a place she had spoken at the year before. I had joined her then as well and watched her deliver an incredible speech that earned her a standing ovation. They had been so impressed that they invited her back as a keynote speaker. Once again, she captivated the audience while I helped set up and cheered her on. Afterward, people approached her to praise her presentation, and many also commented on the unique bond we shared. Spending time together that weekend, discussing my upcoming graduation and our creative ambitions, made different ideas for me, for us, feel more alive than ever.

After Salida, we headed to Vail, where my mom was set to speak at a conference for women lawyers. Just before her presentation, we ran into my former boss—the same person I had worked with to write a sci-fi comic book for preteens that introduced them to God and lessons from the Bible. He knew both me and my mom well, understanding our shared passion for storytelling. As we caught up, I mentioned my senior Capstone project, and he offered a suggestion that struck me: Why not research generational storytelling? Given that my mom and I both tell stories, this theme could provide the perfect bridge between my research and creative components.

The idea intrigued me, but it also felt daunting—writing about storytelling itself was unfamiliar territory.

Later that day, my mom experienced something similar. The audience at the conference wasn't her usual crowd, yet she still delivered a powerful speech. She even mentioned me and our books, and afterward, several attendees approached us to say how inspired they were by our stories and our relationship. It was a weekend filled with creativity, connection, and validation of the very power that is storytelling. Between the conference energy, the unexpected run-in with my boss, and the excitement of people resonating with our journey, it was as if, as we like to quote, "lightning had struck [our] brain." Or, as we also like to say, we had a God moment.

Sitting together in the beautiful hotel in Vail, my mom laid out her brilliant plan.

"We should write a book."

At first, I looked at her like she was crazy—but not for long. The connections, the ideas, and the creativity had been building all weekend. Our relationship had never felt stronger, and so many people had recognized it. I needed a creative component to complement my research on storytelling, and we already had a meaningful foundation—graduating on the same day.

"A memoir—it's perfect," I agreed.

Writing a book in a year felt intimidating, even for me. We still had school, jobs, and a million other responsibilities. But the idea of undertaking a project of this magnitude—one so personal and significant—with my mom thrilled me. We rushed upstairs to a restaurant, ordered a bottle of Prosecco (Mom's favorite), and immediately launched into planning mode. If we were serious, we had to start now. We jotted down ideas, brainstormed the book's theme, and even gave our ambitious plan a code name: "Operation Whistledown"—if you know, you know. As we spoke those words, the bottle of Prosecco popped—literally—and the idea for *Through Her Eyes* was born. My senior project, our next career step, and the continuation of our storytelling legacy were all officially set into motion.

Stories have always been my way of understanding the world—first as a reader, then as a writer, and now as someone shaping a career around them. From the basement computer where I first brought my imagination to life, to the moment I held my own book in my hands, to now embarking on this memoir with my mom, storytelling has been the constant thread woven through every season of my life. It has shaped the way I see myself, the way I connect with others, and the way I move forward. But more than just creating worlds of my own, I want to inspire others—kids, students, dreamers—to believe they can do the same. That they can dream big and accomplish whatever they set their hearts on. All they have to do is start. Nothing would fill me with more joy than knowing that someone read my work, loved it, and walked away believing in their own ability to create. And I owe that dream to my mom because I wouldn't have found it without her.

"My mom taught me a woman's mind should be the most beautiful part of her."
- Sonya Teclai

CHAPTER FIVE

Education

Olivia's Perspective

I was the emcee at a women's founder pitch competition at my alma mater—something I do every year—when a single, off-hand question from another woman backstage reminded me just how loaded the topic of education can be.

The judges and I were gathered behind the curtain, preparing to head out, when she suddenly blurted, "Everyone in this room has an MBA, right?" Her tone was casual. Almost rhetorical. But the words landed like a sucker punch to the chest.

What an odd thing to say, especially considering we each had neatly printed bios in front of us—bios that outlined our career highlights, credentials, and degrees. Why ask something so unnecessary when the answer was literally right in front of her? I don't know if the glance she gave me after that question was coincidental or if I was just being overly sensitive, but I could feel the conversation taking a turn. I knew exactly what that question was implying. And I wasn't ready.

You'd think that with who I am—with the experience I've built, the confidence I carry, the way I show up in a room—I wouldn't get defensive. But I did.

In that moment, my brain scrambled to find an eloquent yet concise response. Something that would call out how irrelevant the question was while also somehow explaining that—though it wasn't on my bio—I had one too.

But the truth?

I didn't.

Not yet anyway.

At the time, I was five weeks shy of receiving my MBA in Entrepreneurship. Five weeks. But standing there, I felt this deep, nagging urge to lie. To say I already had it. To claim that degree even before it was mine. And that made me pause. Why did I feel the need to prove myself?

Maybe because, for the last decade at least, I had been working in—and often leading—rooms full of people with master's degrees. And every time I walked into those spaces, I felt like an underage drinker with a fake ID.

Undercover.

Unqualified.

But willing to let people just assume.

"Passing."

I intentionally didn't get my MBA right out of undergrad because of the brilliant advice from the CEO of the advertising agency I was working at at the time. I owe a lot to him—much more than he knows, I'm sure.

He said, "If you're going to spend the money, have a very good, very specific reason—where you absolutely can't do what you want without it." He was basically saying: Make sure it's not for clout, not for a notch on your belt, and definitely not just because everyone else is doing it.

And I wholeheartedly agreed. I still do.

I've passed along that same advice to so many others: Don't simply get a master's degree because it seems to be the next step, or because of what others may think. Get it because it will unlock something you can't otherwise access.

The other piece of advice he gave me was that, at my young age, I couldn't really make a job decision that would ruin my career. That I had time. I had space. I could pivot.

At the time, I was at a crossroads—overthinking whether to leave the agency for a job that would allow me to spend more time with my tiny, growing family. I was traveling constantly and working long hours, missing critical milestones that I couldn't get back. The pressure and stress started showing up physically—my stomach in knots, my energy drained.

He told me, in his own wise and slightly sarcastic way, to just chill out.

It was only much later that I would realize those early years in my career weren't only about building my resume—they were about building the foundation for the life I wanted down the line. They were purely for me and for my need to be close to these little humans I had created.

As insensitive as it may sound, my babies didn't need me to be there for their first word or first step, or to pick them up every day from daycare. Those moments, while special for me, weren't critical.

What they would need—desperately, deeply—would come much later.

They would need me to be front and center in those middle school and high school years. When they got bullied. When they were called the N-word. When they were first exposed to pornography on a friend's phone. When they lost their first classmate to suicide—yes, *first*, because unfortunately, there would be many. When they suffered their first heartbreak, or came home with tears in their eyes but didn't know how to explain why.

That's when they would need me most.

That's when my job—whatever it was—would need to lend itself to flexibility. The freedom to pick them up early from school. The presence to have the hard conversations. The margin to call in sick just to sit beside them as they cried.

The critical need for freedom would come much later.

But that CEO saw far enough ahead to plant the seed.

I took all the advice he gave me—the job advice, the kids advice, and the MBA advice—to heart. And while it very occasionally came up in my mind or in conversation, I didn't give getting my MBA another thought.

Until I had to.

Mor recently.

For years, I didn't give the MBA another thought. Every so often it would come up in conversation, or cross my mind while updating my LinkedIn profile. But mostly, I was fine without it.

Until things started to shift.

Over the past few years, I've had several opportunities to teach at the collegiate level. I had already been guest lecturing for years—pouring into students, sharing what I'd learned through trial, error, hustle, and Holy Spirit guidance. So when I was approached to teach an actual course—specifically, a personal branding class—I was thrilled.

I was all in.

Because nothing lights me up quite like teaching. Speaking. Guiding young people—especially high school and college students—through the messy beauty of discovering their voice, their purpose, and their power. It's not just work. It's calling.

We moved quickly. Got as far as drafting the course description. Finalizing logistics. They were ready to add my class to the catalog. We were this close.

And then?

They asked for a résumé as a formality. Just a box to check.

I submitted mine confidently.

And that's when I was found out.

No master's degree.

Suddenly, all the years of lived experience, marketing campaigns, branding breakthroughs, startup wins, hard-earned wisdom, and entrepreneurial grit meant... nothing. I was disqualified from teaching a class I had already been teaching in pieces for years—just because I didn't have three extra letters behind my name.

It was embarrassing, to say the least. To get so far into the process... literally to the point where students could register for my class... only to be told I couldn't move forward. I needed more schooling.

So that's what I did.

I went back for the letters.

At first, it was a strategic move. I tried to align myself with a university I had already been deeply embedded in, volunteering my time and guest speaking regularly at their business school. It felt like a win-win for everyone—on paper, at least.

Or so I thought.

When that didn't pan out, I did what any determined woman does when faced with a closed door: I Googled.

I started doing research on Master of Entrepreneurship programs—which, spoiler alert, are few and far between in this country. I even looked into MBAs with a concentration in entrepreneurship—also a short list.

And then, as if divinely placed in the top search results, Belhaven University appeared.

An accredited, online program with a Christian worldview? Check, check, and check.

Google really came through—again. Just like it did when we found Belhaven University for Malia's undergrad a few years prior. We had searched for author scholarships, and there it was. The perfect fit for her.

So, you can imagine my excitement when I realized I might be attending the same university as my daughter. If all things went as planned, we'd be graduating at the same time. Matching cap and gown selfies, here we come.

While I didn't need an MBA to move up or make more money in my current role—the job I loved and had no plan of leaving—I knew I needed the credential to be taken seriously at the university level. Not for the students. Not even for me. But for the gatekeepers. For the systems that still don't see value unless it's stamped on a transcript.

And what I've learned, especially through the lens of being a Black woman, is this: the rules aren't the same for everyone.

Other people—and let's be real here, more specifically white women I know—were being allowed to teach even before they'd completed their master's. One woman even told me, point blank, that she had been teaching at the exact same university I was approached by for years before she ever earned her degree.

It's that subtle but deafening reminder that the bar is just higher for us. That the standard of proof is greater. That excellence, experience, and readiness are not enough when you don't fit the profile of what leadership—or expertise—is supposed to look like.

So, this degree?

It's not just a key for women like me—it's hopefully the unlocking of doors that were already open for others. Doors they've stood outside of for years, knocking with résumés in one hand and results in the other.

It's wild when you think about it. Companies across the country are working, even if passively, to narrow the equity gap. They're hosting summits, launching DEI departments, rolling out glossy campaigns about representation. And yet, when asked why an entire suite or board lacks Black women, the answer is often: "We couldn't find qualified candidates with the right credentials."

But here's the truth: Black women are more likely than any other demographic to earn degrees, including master's degrees.

We're out here. We exist. We are qualified.

So maybe the real question isn't where are we.

Maybe the question is: Where are you looking?

So, while I most likely could have taught most of the classes I took, I still spent two years "learning" about business strategy, marketing and communications, strategic decision-making, entrepreneurship, people management, and entrepreneurial finance. It was less about learning entirely new concepts and more about deepening what I already knew and finally validating the career experience I had accumulated over the years.

And what I learned most was about myself—who I am and what I'm capable of.

I never thought I could go back to school. Not because I didn't want to, but because school was hard for me. It always took a lot of effort. A lot of work. And I honestly wasn't sure if I could keep up—especially after almost failing my very first class simply because I didn't turn things in. That initial wake-up call hit hard.

But I did it.

And I did it alongside Malia.

She became my built-in accountability partner, checking in on me on nights when assignments were due and every weekend when papers needed to be submitted. When she was home for Christmas break, we'd walk to get coffee together and do homework side by side. I was the one who wanted to push things off, shelve it until tomorrow, and suggest we just hang out instead. She's the one who would bring us back on task—reminding me we could hang out once we finished what we had to do.

She kept us going.

And now—graduation.

It worked out so that Malia and I will walk across the same commencement stage, on the same day, in the same ceremony in Jackson, Mississippi—right alongside her friends and peers. Just typing that sentence still feels surreal.

What an accomplishment for both of us—and a testament to God's divine alignment and the unimaginable things you can accomplish when you put your mind (and your heart, soul, and prayers) to it.

Our regalia is ordered, the date is set, and the countdown has begun. Caps, gowns, tassels, and tears.

As we begin to prepare for this incredible milestone, I find myself reflecting on the importance of continuing to learn and grow—not just in the classroom, but in life.

The older I get, the more I realize that graduation isn't a finish line. It's a celebration of how far you've come—and a launching point for everything still ahead.

Do I need a few minutes to recover before I even *think* about teaching a class? Oh absolutely. Maybe more than a few. But just like with any credential, this one gives me something invaluable: choice.

The freedom to say yes. The power to say no. The permission to decide for myself, instead of having a gatekeeper decide for me.

And that right there is what makes the work I do today so personal. So powerful. So necessary.

This is usually where my colleagues would expect me to start quoting the Colorado Pipeline Report. I'll spare you the charts and data, but the bottom line is this: If you want to survive—if you want to thrive, to earn a living wage, to afford rent or a mortgage or raise a family—you're going to need some sort of education or credential after high school.

A high school diploma isn't enough anymore. It's simply not going to cut it.

Which is why, for my kids, the expectation was never "if" you'll pursue something after graduation. It was always "what." You have to choose something. You have to do something. Not because I said so, but because I want you to have options.

I want you to have freedom.

I want you to have the kind of expansive life where you're not stuck choosing between survival and fulfillment. That's what we all deserve.

Education was always a big deal in my family—but in kind of a weird way.

Aside from a year or two of kindergarten in Rochester, New York, before moving to Denver, we were all homeschooled. That made sense—my mom was a former middle school teacher. She had the background, the knowledge, and most importantly, the patience to teach annoying little kids like us. But the catch? She was one of the working moms. Which meant she wasn't exactly available to play the role of full-time educator.

So, our schooling ranged from super-strict, regimented periods of time spent in front of a chalkboard, memorizing U.S. capitals—spitting out Juneau, Boise, Tallahassee like it actually meant something—to memorizing spelling words, and multiplication tables. Then there were various seasons where there were very long stretches of time home alone.

During those stretches of weeks and months, our teachers became the popular soap operas of the '80s and '90s, and our classrooms were the fictitious cities where all the drama unfolded.

Guiding Light was my absolute favorite. From the epic love story of Reva Shayne and Joshua Lewis, to the messy family dynamics of the Bauer's, to the evil schemes of Roger Thorpe—let's just say I got a very early education in lies, deceit, murder, lustful affairs, and people mysteriously coming back from the dead.

It's honestly a miracle that when I finally went to real school in ninth grade, I knew anything at all.

Not only did I manage—I did really well, but I really had to work for it. I kept my head down, stayed focused, and thrived on the satisfaction of checking assignments off the list and turning them in on time.

Who was that girl?

And where is she now?

Some days, she feels long gone. Replaced by an older woman now stuck in her ways—tangled up in painful procrastination, brain fog, forgetfulness, scattered thoughts, time mismanagement, and the occasional bout of functional depression. I feel like I'm constantly fighting her to function at her God-given potential.

And honestly? Some days I don't have the energy to fight.

I suspect it's a combination of the horrendous side effects of perimenopause and the growing realization that I may have been living with undiagnosed ADHD my whole life.

It was when I was trying to help my son manage his own executive dysfunction—just as he was preparing to graduate high school—that it finally hit me. I was watching him struggle, trying to find tools, resources, and support, all while drowning in my own challenges with focus and follow-through. I became desperate. Desperate for him and for me. We needed help.

But the options out there were overwhelming. Endless. And not all of them actually helpful.

That intense problem—the weight of needing support but not knowing where to turn—shaped what would ultimately become the subject of my final thesis for my MBA program: a company designed to intentionally and carefully curate resources for high-performing, entrepreneurial women with ADHD.

It's a business I never intend to launch.

But it was a requirement and a realization I needed to come to— a deep truth I needed to name.

Because I need something to change.

And I know I'm not the only one.

There are so many women out there like me—smart, driven, successful women who've spent their whole lives achieving so much, acting like we have it all together, while quietly falling apart behind the scenes. And they need support, too.

No one really seemed to talk about college growing up. It wasn't a regular dinner table conversation. Ha, we didn't have a regular dinner table or regular dinner table conversations. No one asked, "So, where do you see yourself going to school?" It just wasn't a thing.

But then I remembered my dad—and his infamous, unshakable belief in Harvard. In his mind, Harvard was the pinnacle. The best of the best. And since his kids were clearly the best of the best too, that's where we were going.

But as college got closer, reality set in.

Harvard wasn't going to happen—not just for financial reasons, not just for logistical ones, and not for the fact that my high school guidance counselor didn't even tell me how to apply to an Ivy League school. The dream pivoted. I began setting my sights on what was local and attainable. I applied to every college in Colorado and a few out of state. I got accepted into most. But in the end, I landed in Boulder—for a handful of practical reasons: the close to a full ride need-based and academic scholarships I would receive and the closeness to home.

At that point, it was just me and my mom. My big family had dissolved, many of the moms went their separate ways and I went from one of the oldest of 13 kids to an only child practically over-night. Sad and alone doesn't even begin to describe how I was feeling.

My mom was working full-time and trying to raise a teenage daughter on her own. I didn't understand the full weight of that then, but now—having been a mother myself—I look back in awe at her resilience. Without her sacrifice—her inhuman ability to keep going despite everything life threw her way—I wouldn't be who I am.

But leaving for college?

It took a huge toll on her.

One I didn't fully recognize until many years later. My mom isn't one to talk about her feelings much or wear her emotions on her sleeve especially back then. She didn't tell me what she wished for or what she wanted. Again, as a mom I get it. Those things felt locked up—hidden deep in a vault that neither she nor I had the key to.

I didn't know until she told me—decades later, as I prepared to send my own daughter off to school—just how lonely my leaving had made her feel.

And so, I braced myself when Malia made the decision to move across the country for college.

I tried to act cool and nonchalant. Supportive, encouraging, strong. But inside, I was a weepy mess. Wrestling with the same ache my mom had quietly carried all those years ago. Malia had followed a similar path to mine in many ways—applying to all the local schools first, trying to make the puzzle fit close to home. But because she wanted a degree specific to creative writing, it forced her to broaden her territory.

She applied to countless private schools with impressive writing departments, and as the acceptance letters rolled in, the reality of cost began to hit us in waves.

How were we going to pay for this?

We had no idea.

We barely had money to pay for the place we were living. We had no back up plan. No college savings account waiting in the wings. Just faith. Prayers. And a ridiculous amount of paperwork. This is a problem so many families face—especially those less privileged than ours. You do everything right—prepare your child, encourage their dreams, celebrate the acceptance letter—and then stare at the tuition bill like it's a ransom note.

But somehow, by God's grace, we made it work.

And now?

Now she's about to hold that ridiculously expensive piece of paper in her hand—that I sincerely hope she displays in a ridiculously expensive frame. Because it means something. It means everything.

But here's the real talk: that diploma doesn't mean a job is waiting.

While it helps, it doesn't guarantee financial security. It doesn't promise instant success. What it does is unlock doors. That's it.

It may even open them. But the knocking? The walking through? The courage to even approach the door in the first place?

That part is up to her.

She will have to knock on as many doors as possible. She will have to push through fear, rejection, and disappointment. She will have to step into some rooms boldly and others with trembling hands. And the most beautiful part?

She will also have the freedom and ability to close a door—and simply choose another one.

Because that's what education should give you.

Freedom. Choice.

Not a guarantee—but the power to navigate your own life. To walk your own path. To pivot, to reroute, to pick yourself back up and try again when the first (or fifth) door slams in your face.

And if that's not worth all the late-night papers, the loans, the questionable dorm food, and the stress—we need to rethink what we're telling our kids education is really for.

Because for Malia—and for me—it was never just about the piece of paper.

It's about the power we will now possess.

Malia's Perspective

A lot of times, education has felt like my entire life. When you're in school from kindergarten to twelfth grade, what else is there? From early morning rides to study sessions, the routine of school shaped my days, my friendships, and even my sense of self. But for most of those years, school was a place of joy and excitement. I was the kid who genuinely loved learning—not just the subjects, but the environment, the teachers, the structure. I found comfort in the rhythm of the school day, the way each year brought new lessons, new challenges, and new things to look forward to. Even the little things—picking out new backpacks at the start of the year, sharpening pencils down to tiny nubs, racing to finish multiplication drills—felt like small adventures.

In preschool and kindergarten, I attended a school for gifted children, though I didn't know it at the time. I was just having fun—learning about dry ice, building my own oven to cook pizza, and even making a song in a recording studio. I got to create my own set of drums! Every day felt like an adventure, filled with hands-on experiments and creative projects that made learning feel more like play. I didn't realize that my school experience was any different from anyone else's. To me, it was normal to spend the day exploring new ideas, asking questions, and diving headfirst into projects that made my tiny hands feel capable of big things.

Years later, I found out I had taken a test to get in, and that realization impressed me. At three and four years old, I had already been labeled a "gifted child." Looking back, I don't think I ever felt particularly gifted; I just felt curious. I was eager to learn, to create, to discover. If anything, those early years instilled a love for learning that would follow me for the rest of my life. The confidence I gained from those experiences—being encouraged to try, to explore, to experiment—became a foundation I didn't even know I was building.

From there, I went to a charter school where my dad worked. My eight years there shaped me in ways I didn't fully understand at the time. I met amazing friends, developed a love for learning, and unknowingly started my trajectory toward academic validation.

First grade introduced me to homework, and I wasn't great at it at first. I did the humiliating walk of shame more than once—retrieving forgotten assignments with my dad after school. But when I actually sat down to do my homework, I loved it. No muss, no fuss, and within fifteen minutes, it was done. School itself was just as easy. Math, science, language arts, Spanish—everything clicked. The biggest challenge I faced wasn't grades, but getting in trouble for talking too much in class.

From *gifted child* to *teacher's pet*, I wore all the titles. School was a blast, and good grades came effortlessly. I almost always got As, and each one made my smile bigger. But that love for As slowly became something else. Anything less than perfection sent me into a spiral.

I still remember the exact moment that spiral started. In eighth grade, my Language Arts class read *Inside Out and Back Again* by Thanhha Lai, a verse novel about a ten-year-old girl immigrating to the U.S. in 1975. For our assignment, we had to write a series of poems continuing the story. Poetry wasn't my thing, but something about this project excited me. Maybe more than any other assignment I'd ever received.

131

At the height of my creative imagination—right on the cusp of finishing my first book—my fingers twitched with excitement. Where would I start? What would I say? How would I structure the poem? Hours flew by as I crafted what I believed was my masterpiece. Each line was longer than a typical poem, but I thought that made it unique.

When I turned it in, I was eager to hear my teacher's feedback. At that point, As were second nature. Looking back, part of me wishes I had gotten more Bs and Cs along the way—maybe then I wouldn't have expected perfection. Maybe then I wouldn't have been completely shattered when I got my poem back with a fat, red D.

My whole body went numb. My masterpiece had been reduced to sixty percent. I shoved it in my backpack, afraid it would burn my hands. When I finally looked at the comments, all I saw were words like "too long" and "chunky stanzas." The rest blurred into insignificance. All I could see was that my work was worth a D. Years of climbing higher and higher, fueled by perfect grades, had left me standing on thin ice. My entire identity was riding on that damn A, and the one D was all it took to crack the surface. Ironic how I once thought those As mattered so much, yet the D is the only grade I remember from all of elementary and middle school.

It only got worse from there.

High school started, and my record of straight As convinced me I could handle anything. Honors Diploma Program, Honors English, Honors Algebra, AP Human Geography, Honors Spanish 4— the whole enchilada. Freshman year went smoothly, and I soared.

Literally—our mascot was a raptor. In our Raptor 101 course, we kept track of our grades, and I proudly flashed my column of As.

But then came sophomore year. Honors Geometry. The numbers and letters on the SmartBoard made zero sense to me, and the fear really set in when I wasn't getting good scores on my homework. I wasn't getting As, like I was supposed to. I had no idea what to do, or who to go to. For the first time in my academic career, I wasn't sailing through.

This is where my mom's wisdom came in—wisdom I wasn't ready to hear. "Study," she said. Simple enough, right? Teachers had said it a thousand times before. Study before the test. Study if you don't understand. But I had never studied. Not really. School had always been easy. I did just enough to keep my "perfect" scores.

My mom told me that she hated the students she went to school with that didn't have to work for their A. The idea of her studying for days to ace a test and someone else just waking up to do the same was infuriating. I told her I didn't like those students either, as there were some in my AP classes. But the reality was, I was that student. I had coasted for so long that when I finally hit an academic wall, I didn't know how to climb over it.

Things only spiraled further. I barely scraped by in Geometry with a C. By the time I got to Honors Algebra 2, I was drowning. I failed my first semester junior year. As in, an actual F. My teacher, Mr. Cunningham, pitied me and bumped it to a D. Thank you, Mr. Cunningham, for sparing me the humiliation. But more than that, thank you for sparing me the pain.

Because the pain wasn't just about bad grades. It was about identity. Who was I if I wasn't an A+ student?

Asking for help should've been an obvious solution. Tutoring, my dad (a math teacher), anything to pull my grade up. But I couldn't do it. Asking for help meant admitting I wasn't an A student anymore, and that I didn't know what I was doing. And I didn't know how to be anything else. Anything lower than that convinced me I was a failure or not enough, instead of showing me what I just didn't understand yet.

Over winter break I decided to drop Honors Algebra 2, and tried learning math in the regular Algebra 2 class. Slowly, I started to learn how to study. My parents even made me agree to seek help from my teachers regularly. That choice single-handedly saved my grade, praise the Lord.

Then COVID-19 hit.

Junior year ended with an added pressure of having to learn through the black hole that was Zoom, and senior year dragged on, frustrating and anticlimactic. My College Algebra teacher understood that I just wanted a grade high enough to never look at an equation ever again, and I had two AP classes on top of that. Studying still wasn't second nature, and online learning made everything worse. Looking back, I realize I could have learned so much more if I had been intentional about my education instead of just chasing grades.

That's what my mom had been trying to tell me. Compared to someone like her—who worked for her grades, who truly learned—what had I gained? The high scores I once cherished blur together now. Most of what I learned, I let pass me by. Meanwhile, my mom didn't just collect knowledge; she earned it.

And she still does.

Education isn't just about grades. It's about the wealth of knowledge that you take with you. When it came time to apply for college, my mindset had completely shifted. It felt like a restart, and a chance to learn how to truly earn my education—not just my grades. And pay for it... sorrows, sorrows, prayers.

After discovering my passion for writing, I knew that was the skill I wanted to pursue. Through trial, error, and a freezing-cold college visit in Michigan, I found my way to Belhaven University in Jackson, Mississippi. A writing scholarship under Angie Thomas herself—the author of *The Hate U Give*, a book she first started to write at Belhaven.

This time, I wasn't just chasing an A. I wanted to chase something real.

I had no idea what I was stepping into. Writing had always been my passion, but I had never studied it formally. What did studying stories even look like? However the course would run, I had one goal (other than wanting to make friends): I wanted to learn constantly. I wanted to make use of my time, pour my energy into my craft, and grow from the knowledge of my professors and classmates.

More or less, that's exactly what I did. I worked to become what my mom was and who I wanted to be. Early in my freshman year, I decided to add Biblical Studies and Business Administration minors to my college track, purely out of a desire to learn more. I wanted to study the Bible more deeply and develop business skills that could support my writing. Throughout college, I still got As, and I'm proud of them. But I'm just as proud of my Bs and what I learned from them. Some of my favorite writing assignments didn't receive the best scores, and some of the classes where I earned a B ended up teaching me the most.

One of those classes was Global Perspectives, a requirement for my major that quickly became a joy. The textbook was almost thicker than my own book, *The Camp Signal*, but it was the first time I fully committed to diving into the material instead of taking shortcuts. That class became my favorite of my entire college career. By the time I started my final courses, I had finally achieved a semester with a 4.0 GPA. As happy as I was, it wasn't everything. Next to the As, I saw the classes I took and the lessons I carried from them. I had grown from being an A+ student to a failing student to, finally, a growing student.

College was a whirlwind of growth, challenges, and discovery. I navigated classes, late-night study sessions, and the balancing act of academics, friendships, and personal development. By the halfway point, I thought I had settled into my college journey. But one conversation that summer changed everything.

My mom talked with me about my junior year and my next steps, but what I never expected to discuss was my mom's next steps. When she told me she wanted to get her master's, I was shocked—but immediately supportive. Her reasons made perfect sense, and when Belhaven became an option, I was biased in the best way. What a story, right? My mom and I attending the same college, without that ever being the plan? But dreams aside, money was as much a factor for her as it was for me, so she explored all her options. She researched, considered her list of colleges, while I hoped to all things Blazer that she would become one. In all seriousness, though, I prayed she would find the program that was right for her, just as she had prayed for me.

As August approached and I packed my bags, the decision was made—my mom was going to Belhaven! I was over the moon, especially after doing the math and realizing that if we both stayed on track, we would graduate on the same day, in the same ceremony. Once I settled back into Jackson, she started her first class, adding a new layer to my college experience, one I never would have imagined. We weren't just mother and daughter; in a way, we became classmates. Though on different academic paths, we suddenly shared the pressures of deadlines, the exhaustion of late nights, and the excitement of learning. It was surreal to check in on each other's due dates and encourage one another through essays and exams. Apart and together, we were both working hard toward degrees that reflected our passions and ambitions.

Now, as we reach the final stretch—graduating together—I cannot explain how excited and grateful I feel. I'm getting to cross an item off my bucket list that I never thought would even be there. It has been such a blessing to witness my mom set a goal and go for it, despite all the risks. As a mom, a full-time employee, and someone with countless responsibilities, she took on her master's with so much empowerment and grace.

I don't think anything could represent our relationship more than graduating together. Yes, she is my mom, and I'm her ridiculous daughter, but we support one another—she is truly my best friend.

College has been about growth, not just for me, but for both of us. Experiencing college with my mom has been one of the most inspiring parts of this journey. She has worked so hard—for this degree, for me, and for the life she has built. Her testimony is unlike any other. She has sacrificed dreams to take care of me while also teaching me the importance of pursuing my own.

Now, as we prepare to walk across the stage, this moment isn't just about individual achievement. It's about a shared milestone—a testament to resilience, hard work, and the bond we've strengthened along the way. My journey through school has been one of growth, discovery, and learning to embrace both challenges and successes. And in college, my mom's return to education has been a powerful reminder that it's never too late to pursue what you want to gain in life. Education isn't just about grades or degrees—it's about the journey, the perseverance, and the people who walk alongside you.

EDUCATION – MALIA

139

"Even if the whole world was throwing rocks at you,
if you had your mother at your back, you'd be okay.
Some deep-rooted part of you would know
you were loved. That you deserved to be loved."
- Jojo Moyes

CHAPTER SIX

Love

Olivia's Perspective

I recently read a quote that said, "Your marriage will be your children's first love story."

While this may be true to some extent, I believe the most impactful love story—the one that truly imprints on them—is the love that parents give to their children. It is the first love story they experience firsthand, the foundation upon which they will build their understanding of love, security, and self-worth.

This could explain so much about the way I once viewed love—what I thought it was, what I thought it wasn't, and ultimately, what I settled for. I grew up with a definition of love that felt flat. One-dimensional. Tainted in some ways.

Until I became a parent.

Before I became a mom, I don't think I truly understood what love really meant.

A parent's love for their child is a powerful, deep, and unconditional bond that shapes a child's sense of self and their ability to form meaningful relationships. It is the first example of love they know, and it seeps into every part of them—how they trust, how they connect, how they see their worth.

Parental love is unwavering. It doesn't rely on perfection or performance. It transcends time, tantrums, and teenage attitude. It remains steadfast, even when things get hard.

When I saw each of my children's faces for the first time, there was an instant, indescribable love that existed—not because of anything they had done, but simply because of who they were to me.

The assignment.

They were brought forth on this planet and placed under my care. Simply by that assignment, I felt love for them.

And yet, nothing could have prepared me for how that love would stretch me, challenge me, or break me open in ways I didn't even know were possible.

There is a saying; *"When you have a child, it's like your heart is walking around outside your body."*

This could not be more accurate.

Parenting is an exercise in love and vulnerability, a constant state of concern and surrender. You pour everything into them, knowing that one day, they will walk into a world you cannot control. You do your best, pray over them, teach them, guide them—but ultimately, you have to let them go.

And that? That is harder than hard.

New parents, the ones just embarking on this wild and unpredictable journey, often respond with excitement when they learn about my *empty nester-ish* status. Their eyes light up, hopeful, as if I've unlocked some secret stage of life they can't wait to get to.

"It must be great that they can take care of themselves. I can't wait until this gets a little easier."

I smile. Should I dash their dreams now, or just wait until they find out?

Sometimes, I let them have their moment of blissful ignorance. Other times, I offer the simple truth:

"Parenting doesn't ever get easier, it just gets different."

I used to think the hardest part of parenting was surviving the sleepless nights, the teething, the tantrums. I thought it was all about making sure they ate their vegetables, learned their ABCs, and didn't grow up to be *that* kid who threw tantrums in the cereal aisle.

But some of my most challenging and heartbreaking parenting moments have been in recent years. Watching them navigate loss, depression, rejection, and failure.

Instead of being up all night with a sick toddler, you're up all night sick to your stomach about your kid not wanting to live.

Instead of rocking them to sleep, you're praying they make it back home safe.

Instead of fixing their boo-boos with a Band-Aid and a kiss, you're holding them as they cry over a heartbreak that no amount of motherly love can mend.

This is the part they don't tell you about in the parenting books. This is the part that leaves you breathless. This is the part that will break you in ways you never saw coming.

And yet, you wouldn't trade it for anything.

Sadly, Malia and her brother have watched me go (and grow) through heartbreak and divorce—twice.

They have seen me love. They have seen me lose.

They have seen me build and rebuild, stand and crumble, laugh and weep.

And maybe, just maybe, there is something beautiful in that.

Because while I never wanted my daughter to witness heartbreak, I also never wanted her to believe in the fairytale version of love that so many of us were sold as young girls. The kind that promises happily ever after without ever explaining what happily actually requires.

I wanted her to know that love is beautiful—but it is also work. That love can heal—but it can also wound.

That love is not something to find—it's something you choose, over and over again.

And most importantly?

That real love, the kind worth waiting for, will never require you to shrink yourself down.

> It will never ask you to be less.
> It will never make you question your worth.
> It will never ask you to endure pain in the name
> of patience.

And that is a lesson I had to learn the hard way.

Through it all, my children have been my greatest teachers. They have shown me the depth of love. They have revealed the power of resilience. They have reminded me, time and time again, that no matter how much the world may change, one truth remains:

We are not meant to do life alone.

And while I may not have always gotten love *right* in the ways I hoped, there is one thing I have done right.

I have loved my children fully. Fiercely. Without condition.

That is the greatest gift I can give them. And it is the greatest gift I hope they carry with them—always.

Malia was six years old when her dad and I separated. We thought we could disguise the change in our lives, pull the wool over the eyes of a girl who had tested high on her IQ test and was excelling at a gifted elementary school. One of our *brilliant* ideas was to order a children's book about separation and divorce—something to gently explain what it meant and prepare her for living in two different homes.

When the book arrived, her dad and I agreed we would sit down and all read it together. I placed it on the kitchen countertop before going to bed, but I lay awake all night thinking about how she would respond in the morning.

Malia, being Malia, got up before us—as she often did—went downstairs, and found the book. Before I could even make it out of bed, she had already read the entire thing. *Several times over.*

What an amateur move, I thought.

Instead of shock or sadness, she simply wanted to know when she was going to get her *new room* and was excited at the thought of having *two* bedrooms to herself.

We made it so that transitions were seamless. Weekends were shared. Even the house we lived in—we swapped staying there so nothing would disrupt the kids' habits and day-to-day life.

This only lasted so long. Eventually, the formal divorce happened, and we got separate places.

In my overprotective and overly optimistic nature, I worked hard to shield my kids from the reality of what was happening. From the emotions I was feeling.

This was the beginning of my obsession with disco balls.

Because when you're having dance parties with your little kids, it's hard to cry. It's hard to be sad.

In our new place, we began a tradition—morning dance parties before school, complete with a rotating disco ball and lights in the dining room. Then a pre-bedtime dance party. A Saturday morning dance party. A "good job at school" dance party. An afternoon "just because" dance party.

My disco ball collection grew.

And so did my ability to mask my emotions.

If I was fine, and I *acted* like everything was fine, my kids would be fine.

That became the unspoken rule.

This coping mechanism would prove to be damaging in the future—for myself and for them.

My message to my kids? *Life is a party. Just keep dancing. Everything's fine.*

Except…it wasn't.

At this point in my life, I was trying to keep it together while running a successful and growing children's clothing line. I was also beginning to mentor a large group of women who had launched mom-and-baby companies around the same time, helping them with marketing, branding, and PR.

But I had hit such a low emotionally that I could barely keep it all together.

I wasn't keeping up on orders.

I wasn't keeping up as a mom.

One morning—one of many mornings when I couldn't get out of bed—Malia came into my bedroom.

"Mommy, Mommy, get up! We're hungry. Me and Baby Gabie need something to eat," she pleaded.

And for the life of me, I couldn't.

I laid there, staring at the ceiling, knowing something had to change immediately.

I turned to a high school friend who was now a doctor. She convinced me that going on antidepressants wasn't a sign of weakness—that depression has real, damaging physical impacts, and that my kids deserved a mom who was functioning and present.

At the time, I was conflicted. I had grown up believing that prayer could solve most anything. If something wasn't working, it was because I wasn't praying hard enough.

And my mom reiterated this dangerous belief constantly.

I could hear her voice. "We just need to pray."

But here's the thing—

Prayer wasn't making breakfast.

Prayer wasn't fulfilling T-shirt orders.

And in the moment, prayer wasn't paying my bills.

It was my *love* for my kids that gave me the strength—though minimal—to push through that rock-bottom time.

It wasn't overnight, but little by little, I made some tough decisions. I shifted my focus from my business back to my career.

I rebuilt my life.

This meant a new job. A new place to stay. A new car. New routines. It also meant *new fears*.

New shame. New negative mindsets.

What was I if I wasn't a wife? Who was I without this person in my life?

I fell in love with Malia's dad at 18, towards the end of my freshman year in college. For ten years, we worked in partnership to build our little life and our little family.

Yes, things had gotten hard. Bills, youth ministry, raising kids—it had all put a strain on us. We had grown distant.

But I still thought we were a good *team*.

Sadly, teammates don't always operate as *life partners*.

And in that moment, when I realized his heart was already decided, I would've done anything to make it work.

But love, as I would come to learn over and over again, cannot be forced.

Though I was single, I never fully operated as a single parent. Malia's dad is literally one of the best dads I've known, so single never meant alone. He is an incredible father.

Thank you, Lord!

It's important to *not* procreate with the wrong person—one of several decisions I am proud of.

Malia's dad was thoughtful enough to give me a *heads-up* just before proposing to his girlfriend. He didn't want me to find out from our kids.

At a young age, they had *great* intentions but also talked *a lot*. It was inevitable that they would come rushing home, bursting with ridiculous amounts of excitement and glee, to share the *crushing* news—completely unaware of how much it made my heart hurt.

I cried for days.

As if I was attempting to release the last bit of grief I had held onto from the loss of the relationship. I didn't want my marriage back. I just wanted to be happy too.

I was glad that he was happy, and in the same shallow breath between cries, devastated that he had moved on and I hadn't.

Every other week, Malia and her brother would return home after spending seven days with their new family. And each time they came back, for the first two or three straight days, I had to endure the gut-wrenching sound of them accidently calling me her name then correcting themselves.

The sound was a constant reminder of how I had failed to keep my marriage, my family, and my life together. By the time that habit wore off, it was pretty much time for them to go back to their dad's only to return and repeat the cycle.

But Malia's stepmom would quickly become the piece of the love story where God would take what fell apart and use her as the glue that would put it back together.

Malia and I often talk about the blessing that she was and continues to be in all of our lives. And the fact that as parents, we can—and always have—put the kids first. Thank you, Lord!

In my singleness, I found myself on a journey to figure out *who* I was in my 30s.

Who I wanted to be.
What I enjoyed doing.

Yoga and roller skating became critical to my sanity during that time.

You see, they both take a certain level of focus and concentration that wouldn't allow my mind to wander or overthink too much.

I was also in a phase where I needed to *prove* to myself that I was pretty. That I was *sexy* and *desired*.

That phase only lasted ten months or so, and while it left my confidence high, it left my self-worth extremely low.

Not quite five years had gone by before I met what was supposed to be the next love of my life.

God speaks to us in very mysterious ways—usually never directly, and never in the way I would prefer it.

I've only heard God speak clearly a handful of times in my life. And this time, I would never forget.

During an all-night prayer, a man that I had seen a handful of times but never really spoken to started walking my way, and God very clearly said—

"You'll look back on this day and remember that this was the day I would introduce you to your husband."

Note that there was no timing or timeline.

> No explanation.
> No clarity.
> No instructions to take any action.

A year would pass before we even spoke again.

And just over another year before we got married.

The entire time leading up to our wedding day was filled with lapses in communication, uncertainty, dishonesty, and resentment.

The only thing I knew for sure were the words that God spoke to me several years prior.

At the time, my faith in God and my love for God fueled my faith and love for this man.

Even when nothing else made sense.

A year would pass before we spoke again, and just over another year before we got engaged then married. The entire time leading up to our wedding day was filled with lapses in communication, uncertainty, dishonesty, and confusion. The only thing I knew for sure were the words that God had spoken to me several years prior.

My faith in God and my love for God fueled my faith and love for this man.

Prior to our wedding day, our relationship had remained some sort of a secret to those in our church for many reasons.

I asked him two weeks before our wedding if he was going to change his single status on social media to "married".

The only reason I asked this question was because we had already gone through issues with lies and misrepresentations involving other women online, and I wanted to go into the marriage with open communication and transparency.

His response was shocking and beyond defensive.

He got so angry at the question that it threw him into a raging fit of anger.

It happened following a small engagement dinner that a friend had thrown for us. I was driving on the highway, and I could barely keep the car on the road due to the screaming, threatening and intimidating physical movements, and gestures being thrown my way from the passenger seat.

I could feel his breath as his face was an inch from my ear, screaming profanities and calling me a bitch for asking him such a pointless and insecure question. He started punching the dashboard and suddenly opened the car door—at a speed of at least 55 mph.

I pulled over, barely keeping control, and he jumped out and started walking toward oncoming traffic.

I was crying. Shaking. Asking God, *Are you sure?*

In my many, many prayers and questioning, God never directly responded with an "*I'm sure*".

But I kept hearing, *"This is My son. Don't give up on him."*

I took those words to heart, and every time I heard them, I would double down on my faith, love, and loyalty.

While this was the first incident of anger and rage I had experienced, it wouldn't be the last.

Six months in, and on Valentine's Day, I let my youngest sister know I needed to stay with her and my mom for a day or two. Earlier that day my ex-husband was getting texts from a woman that included explicit details of their activities together and nude pictures.

I confronted him, holding back tears.

Two hours later, what remained were broken picture frames, bedsheets and blankets thrown all over the bedroom, bruising on my arms and around my neck, and a scared Malia in the other room who was awakened by my screams.

For me, cheating didn't necessarily mean the end. What about grace and forgiveness? Second chances? But when I didn't choose to leave him at that moment, my relationship with my sister suffered the consequences. We didn't speak for over two years. She had the tendency to write long messages or emails to people when it called for a conversation. She hadn't had a long-term relationship, she was never married, and she didn't have kids. So I decided she didn't know what she was talking about. Looking back, I was wrong, but blind faith kept me there. To my sister, I'm sorry. You were right.

For close to 10 years and after at least 5 second chances, I would see this side of him many times, all pointing back to addiction, dishonesty, and infidelity.

I married Dr. Jekyll. And I truly loved him—the beautiful, intricate pieces of him and the broken, messy ones as well.

And had to face the recurring consequences of Mr. Hyde—

In our home.
In our finances.
In our business.
In our bedroom.
In our family.

Our wedding day was beautiful. And in some ways it was the beginning of something beautiful... and toxic.

Super small and intimate, with only about twenty folding chairs filled with family in the park behind my mom's house.

A gorgeous white Pottery Barn chandelier adorned the tree where we stood and said our vows. Promises that we couldn't keep.

My son walked me down the aisle, while Malia and my ex-husband's daughter escorted him towards me.

I had no clue what I was walking into.

What I would put my kids through.

In hindsight, do I believe I made a horrible mistake?

Not necessarily.

I do believe that the journey I've had has made me the woman I am—in all of its glory, tragedy, intricacies, beauty, and mess. I believe I lived in complacency, passivity, and avoidance—under the guise of faith.

Today, I stand in the midst of the wreckage of my decisions, my actions, and my denial—fully aware of how those decisions shifted the path of my life, had a hand in failed marriages, tarnished the example of love that I showed my kids, and warped how I view any possibility of love in the future.

This past year, I've become terribly aware of how coping methods and defense mechanisms can twist and pervert how you see yourself and how you project yourself onto others.

How I perceive, receive, and give love will forever be shaped by the love I did and didn't receive from the men in my life, my father included.

The beauty and hope in all of this is that I have an opportunity to redefine love—through the eyes of God, the Creator of love.

This is no simple task.

And it may take the rest of my lifetime to achieve.

Enter *the man in the grey hat*!

A larger-than-life example of love, surrender, and realness that I didn't want, didn't ask for, and most certainly wasn't prepared for. But he barged into my world riding gold turntables and extending his hand during the most painful couple years of my life.

He appeared completely out of nowhere—both random and undeniably and divinely assigned at the same time. We had briefly crossed paths at a high school friend's wedding, and then, after a casual text exchange well over a year later, he resurfaced.

I tried my best to put him off. I took days—weeks even—to respond to his texts. I dismissed his attempts to connect. I even flat-out told him that I wasn't interested in a relationship and that I had absolutely nothing to offer anyone in my current state of hurt, de-pletion, and exhaustion. I was in the thick of it—navigating a new life in a new apartment, navigating a divorce that would take several sharp, painful turns for the worst. I was rebuilding my life from the rubble and mourning the loss of what I had believed, for so long, was God's promise.

He was understanding, but he was also persistent.

I told him, very clearly, "I just need some time to heal alone."

And with what I now recognize as stubborn boldness, and di-vine determination (or foolishness), he replied,

"Why not heal with me?"

Excuse me, sir? You don't know me. You definitely don't know what I need. And you absolutely don't know what I've been through.

But... after a couple sessions of spending hours on the phone, I started to get a glimpse into the man in the grey hat—all of his beauty, his brilliance, his brokenness, and all of his complexities. The way his mind worked, the way he listened and asked the hard questions, the way he reflected things back to me that I hadn't even realized about myself—it was disarming and alarming.

I wasn't ready for this.

He asked me out on a formal date. And when I say formal, I mean formal.

He didn't slide into my DMs with a "wyd?" or hit me with a "Let's link." No, he asked if I would have dinner with him and if I was available on a specific day and at a specific time. Then he followed up to ask about any food allergies. He made restaurant reservations (I know right) at an incredible spot that catered to my vegetarian needs. And before I even arrived, he made sure valet parking was arranged.

I was blown away, to say the least.

It was such a clear reflection of how he approaches all things—with care, with detail, with intention and a little bit of obsession. But it was also a stark contrast, a jarring comparison, to how I had been treated in the past. It stirred up emotions I didn't know I still had tucked away.

When I arrived at the restaurant, the hostess knew exactly who I was and ushered me up to the rooftop through a private elevator. I was greeted by name—again—and brought to a secluded corner table where a man in a grey hat sat with his back to me, facing the window and the breathtaking city skyline.

My heart pounded as I approached.

We were both nervous, our laughter slightly too loud at first, our voices fumbling over each other. We ordered frozen rosé and paella—so much paella that I literally ate it as leftovers for the rest of the week.

When dinner was over, he offered to drive me to my car.

I immediately brushed it off. "My car is only two blocks away", I explained.

In hindsight, this was the very beginning of his endless attempt to be a much-needed protector and provider in my life. And it was also the beginning of my unfortunate habit of repeatedly denying him that opportunity.

He insisted.

And when he opened his car door a massive, vibrant bouquet of flowers was waiting in the passenger seat.

I held back tears and felt silly getting emotional on a first date. I had been through a lot. I was going through a lot. But this? This was the beginning of something deeper. The beginning of feeling emotionally vulnerable... and eventually safe. The beginning of learning what it could mean to be seen and loved well.

Over the course of the next year and a half, I've laughed more than I've ever laughed in my life. Like, face-hurting, belly-grabbing, can't-catch-my-breath kind of laughter. He's shown me a kind of love, care and intentionality that I didn't know I needed, and it has even extended to my kids. That part alone? Wow.

The man in the grey hat has held up a mirror to me—revealing the most incredible and unique parts of who I am. But also, the most ugly and bruised. The most guarded. The parts I'd rather not look at much less reveal to others—the ones still harboring pain, fear, resentment, and self-doubt. The parts that have learned to push people away in an attempt to survive rather than live.

Despite how many times I've tried to push him away—whether out of fear or habit—he remains steady, a rock.

Steadfast.

Broken in his own right.

And yet, unbreakable.

Just like that, I was falling. In a very grounded, eyes wide open, reality-based way. No butterflies. Just certainty.

I've never been in a relationship where I had so much to learn, and where I wasn't the one always doing the teaching. That alone was humbling. He's younger than me, but somehow his wisdom carries the weight of someone who's lived many more lifetimes. Never having been married, and without kids of his own, he has still managed to be one of the most grounded, insightful people I've ever met.

That said—his temperament and delivery?

Let's just say, there's room for growth and interpretation.

The way he gives direction, the way he offers provision, the way he tells me what I *should* be doing? It frequently rubs me the wrong way and makes it hard to receive—because I'm not used to receiving. I'm used to *being* the one.

> The one that provides.
> The one that guides.
> The one that protects.
> The one that makes things happen.

So, yes. Letting go of that control is one of the hardest things. And opening myself up to the possibility of being hurt again? Also, one of the hardest things.

But this love was worth it.

Every single day, I thank God for this unexpected chapter. For this single season, with him in my life and by my side.

To be deeply loved by the man in the grey hat?

There's absolutely nothing like it.

The way he sees me. Holds space for me. Challenges me. Covers me. The way he's willing to weather the storm with me and not just stand in the sunshine. It's the kind of love that I pray rewires me. The kind that will soften me where I've been hardened and affirms what my past has tried to strip away. It's not perfect—and neither are we—but it's real.

And yet...

To be truly loved by myself?

That's the love story I'm still learning how to write.

A love that doesn't wait for someone else's confirmation. A love that doesn't shrink in the face of rejection. A love that doesn't depend on who texts back or who chooses me. A love that starts within and radiates out—not the other way around.

That's the love story that will change everything. The one I want to show my kids.

What a magical, sacred, and deeply personal love story it will be—when I fully step into the fierce, unapologetic adoration and protection of myself. Prioritizing, above all else, my own well-being, joy, softness, power, and peace. Not out of bitterness, not out of ego, not out of fear, but out of reverence.

Because I deserve to be held by myself the way I've held everyone else.

Because little Olivia—the girl with the stiff hair, the paper dolls, and the quiet longing to belong—deserves to be protected by grown-up Olivia.

This is the part where I show my kids what love looks like in its truest form: not just romance or partnership, but full recognition and appreciation for my own self-worth. Treating myself like I would treat my daughter, my son, my best friend. Saying yes to what lights me up. Saying no, boldly and without guilt, to what dims me.

This is where I finally tell the little girl in me:

You are enough.
You always were.
You belong everywhere you are.

As an adult, I spent years believing that belonging meant blending in. Going with the flow. Not rocking the boat. Keeping quiet when something didn't feel right. Smiling when I wanted to scream. Nurturing others while neglecting myself.

Even if it meant denying who I was.

Even if it meant abandoning what I needed. Even if it meant shrinking for the sake of someone else's comfort.

But now? Now I know better.

Now I'm learning that true love isn't found in sacrificing your wholeness for someone else's ease. It's found in honoring the divine within you—the version of you that God so carefully and intentionally crafted. The version that doesn't need to perform or prove, but simply be.

Now that's a love story I'll be proud to share.

With my kids. With the world.

And most importantly, with myself.

Malia's Perspective

Love was simple and beautiful at first—a chaotic mixture of my mom, my dad, my brother, and me, dancing and singing in the White House. I know what you're thinking, and no, I'm not Malia from the White House. Crazy. White House was what my family and I called the white townhome we lived in together, with our scary basement and (my) bins of dress-up costumes. That was what love was—just a house, a family of four who loved each other.

I was seven, and I remember waking up and feeling like something was off. It probably wasn't a school morning because the morning was moving very slowly. I walked downstairs into the living room, no one else was awake. There was a book sitting on the couch, one I hadn't seen before. I've done some research, and I'm like 99% sure the book was called Dinosaurs Divorce: A Guide for Changing Families by Marc Brown. I remember because when I opened the book and flipped to a page, it landed on an illustration of a little girl dinosaur with each parent on either side of her. Sitting at their feet was a pile of dolls and other toys, and below it, the caption explained that you could divide your toys so some could be at each house. My face crinkled as I read the words. Each house? Why would some of my toys not be with me?

By then, my body had lowered onto the couch, the house even quieter as I flipped through more pages—one about different ways parents fight, another showing a parent driving away. There was this word that kept repeating itself throughout the book. Divorce. What does that mean?

By then, my mom had found me. I don't remember what was said, but she was very calm when she said it. Something along the lines of my brother and I spending some time with her at a different house. My face crinkled again. Why would we go somewhere else when all of our stuff was here? What about Dad?

Childhood is a messy painting with a lot of scattered blobs of paint, memories blending into one another. So next thing I remember, Mom had already moved away. I was with her, my brother, and my grandma at her house, probably eating dinner. I was sad—crying, in fact. I missed my dad, and I couldn't understand why he wasn't there. I asked Mom if I could call him, and as soon as she dialed, the phone was in my hands.

"Can I see you?" I asked.

"You can see me next week when you come over," he answered.

My tears fell harder. While I didn't understand much, my heart sank to my feet. Coming over to him suddenly meant leaving my mom behind. I just wanted to have dinner with both of them, like we used to. When did love become a choice between two people? Why couldn't I just have them both at the same time?

"I want us to all be together."

There was a long silence on the other end.

"I know, sweetheart."

The phone was passed back to Mom. I sat there, staring at my plate, trying to make sense of why love—something I thought was supposed to mean staying—felt so much like leaving. It felt like love had rules I didn't know about—rules that could be broken. Why did love come with conditions?

At seven, I didn't have the words to ask that question, but I felt it pressing against my heart. Love started to feel uncertain, fragile—something that could be here one moment and gone the next. But just as I was beginning to believe love meant leaving, someone new arrived.

For a while, it was just the three of us—Dad, my brother, and me. Mornings were early so he could get us to school before heading down the hallway to teach his students. Sundays weren't for church but for library visits, wandering through rows of books and playing computer games. Our nights were filled with movies—The Avengers on repeat—park visits, and silly dinner conversations. Life was small but full, just us three.

Then, one day, we went to the park and met some people there. A pretty woman, a teacher I recognized from my school, stood under a tree with a little boy, maybe two years old. She was nice—the kind of nice that made me feel safe. My brother and I ran off to the playground with the little boy, but I kept glancing back at my dad and her, standing close, talking in a way that wasn't just friendly. I smiled to myself, maybe even giggled.

Gradually, she and the little boy started appearing in our lives more and more—movies, board games, snowball fights. We had big sleepovers, all five of us crammed together, and it was so much fun.

Then, one day in our apartment, my dad called the three of us—me, my brother, and the little boy—into his room. He grinned, that infamous grin of his, and pulled out a small black box. Inside was a ring. A ring. I gasped, eyes wide. He didn't let me scream, but I wanted to.

They were getting married! We were going to be a family.

The wedding came in January, just before I turned ten. I was overjoyed, ready to tell the world about my new mom and my new brother.

But then something weird happened. She actually became my mom.

What followed that amazing day were months of arguments, bitter conversations, and plenty of attitude—entirely on my part. If you had asked me then why I was so angry, I wouldn't have had an answer. I just was. Writing furious entries in my diary, creating problems where there weren't any, making life harder for the woman who had only ever loved me.

Looking back, I'm not proud of that season. But now, watching my brother and stepmom's relationship grow, I see what happened. The truth was, from the moment my dad got married, I gained a new mother figure. But I already had a mom. Adding another piece to my family felt strange. Uncomfortable. I didn't know where to put it, or how to describe it.

This woman wasn't my mom, but she was in a mom role. She picked me up from school, made me dinner, and told me what to do. She changed my life, and at the time, I didn't know how to handle that. I thought there could only be one mom, and I didn't want to betray the one I already had.

But love has a way of settling in quietly, making room where you don't realize it.

One night, after dinner had been eaten and it was time for bed, my stepmom said goodnight to my brothers before coming into my room, snuggling in beside me. Nestled in her arms, I told her about school, my classmates, the things I was thinking about. She told me about the books she was teaching her students, and I told her what book I wanted to read next. She listened and held me and laughed with me. I scratched her back, and she kissed my head. With her, nothing bad could happen to me. Cuddles in the morning, cuddles at night—I had found another person to hold my joys and dreams. My mom.

Slowly, that strange, unfamiliar piece became a perfect fit—one I hadn't even realized I was missing. I can't imagine my life without her now.

Love comes into your life in different ways, looking different each time. But it never takes away what was there before—it only adds to it. Over time, love took on new meanings. It wasn't just about who stayed or who left—it was about the choices people made to build something together. Not long after my stepmom joined our family, another change was on the horizon. Within the year, my mom was also getting married.

I was over the moon. A stepfather, a new brother, a new sister—my family was growing again. But with all the excitement came a nervous energy that I didn't quite know what to do with. Two blended families felt like a lot. Everything I had known and understood about my family was shifting, and now, adjusting to two different households felt like I had nowhere steady to land.

The afternoon before the big day, my mom and I were in the car, talking about wedding plans as we drove past the park by my grandma's house—the place where the ceremony would be. I stared out the window at the familiar trees, now holding a new kind of significance. I turned to her.

"How do you feel?" I asked.

She smiled, her hands steady on the wheel. "I feel good. Calm."

I frowned. "Why? I thought you'd be nervous."

She told me that a long time ago, she was in church praying, and when he walked past her, God said, "That is your husband."

I stared at her, letting the words settle. This day had been planned long before I even knew to be excited about it. I smiled then, in awe.

The wedding day arrived, and I was ecstatic. I loved weddings— the dresses, the flowers, the feeling of something new and a magical beginning. And this time, it was my mom's happy ending.

I got ready with my soon-to-be stepsister, both of us in white, mirrors reflecting our exhilaration. I only saw my mom's makeup before we left for the park, anticipation buzzing as I imagined her in the dress.

Guests arrived, filling the space with chatter and laughter. The air was warm, thick with summer and expectation. As the service began, I took my position with my stepsister and stepfather-to-be. We linked arms, exchanging wide grins before stepping forward.

The grass was soft beneath our feet as we walked triumphantly down the aisle, bathed in golden sunlight. Beneath the chandelier hanging from the tree, we reached our place and she and I found our seats at the front. And then, my breath caught.

There she was.

My mom, radiant in white, moving gracefully down the aisle with my brother by her side. My vision blurred as tears welled up. The weight of the moment settled in—it was happening. This new beginning, this love, was real.

The ceremony was beautiful, but one moment took my breath away. My mom and her soon-to-be husband removed their shoes, bent down, and began to wash each other's feet.

I cried then, watching something truly magical unfold. Two people, vowing not just to love each other but to serve one another. The act was quiet, yet it spoke volumes.

At that moment, I knew—one day, at my own wedding, I wanted to do the same.

That day, I saw love as something heavenly. Something that could be found again in new seasons, written into our lives by the One who plans them long before we even know to dream.

As I got older, love wasn't just something I saw in weddings or heard in vows—it was also in the quiet, everyday moments between people who chose to show up for each other. Before I ever learned what love looked like in romance, I found it in friendship.

I met them in youth group—the three girls who quickly became my best, best friends. From the very first sleepover, where we belted out ballads on the kitchen floor and had whipped cream fights until we were breathless with laughter, I knew we had something special. We did everything together—whispered about crushes at midnight, planned our futures, and promised to always be there for each other. I never questioned it. In my mind, we were forever.

When COVID-19 happened, I thought the distance would be hard on all of us. But something felt off. The group chat, once alive with our endless jokes, became silent. I would try to revive it, sending messages asking how they were. The responses were short, if they even came at all. My heart sank. Had I done something wrong?

When restrictions were lifted enough for us to see each other again, I was desperate to show them how much I cared. I drove all over town, dropping off little gifts for each of them. I waited for their excitement, their thank-yous, something to reassure me that we were still us. But my phone stayed quiet.

One day, a Snapchat notification lit up my screen. I opened it eagerly, my heart leaping at them reaching out. But my excitement turned to ice as I stared at the picture. It was of the three of them, smiling, laughing, and sitting on a picnic blanket. Without me. They hadn't invited me.

I didn't respond. What was I supposed to say? I slowly put my phone down, my chest aching. They must have forgotten, I told my-self. I was still their friend... wasn't I?

When youth group finally resumed in person, I was thrilled at the thought of seeing them again. I walked in, scanning the room for my girls, ready to finally fall back into our rhythm. But they were already deep in conversation, talking about plans I hadn't heard of, about people I didn't know. I sat with them, trying to find my way back into the space that used to be mine, but I could feel it slipping further away. Every week, the distance grew. The texts got shorter, and their whispered conversations got longer.

One night, they arrived late, laughing as they carried their Starbucks cups. No one had even told me they were going or asked if I wanted anything. That night, I sat away from them, not wanting to fight for a space they had decided I didn't belong in anymore.

After youth group ended, one of them finally texted, asking if we could all talk. My heart pounded as we stepped outside to the swings. Maybe this was it. Maybe they had noticed and could fix it. I swallowed my fear and told them the truth—I felt alone. I felt left out. I didn't know how to fit in anymore. I had missed them, and I didn't understand what was happening. Please see me, your friend.

The girl who had sent the text stared at me, confused. Then, she spoke:

"That's not our fault."

What followed wasn't an apology. It wasn't an under-standing. It was a performance—a carefully crafted monologue about how it was my responsibility to stay included, how they weren't to blame for my feelings, how I just needed to do more. As if I hadn't already spent months trying. As if I hadn't already begged for them to see me. I thought being loved by people was supposed to mean honesty, but when I asked them for the truth, all I got were excuses that made me the problem.

I felt the tears spill over as the other two sat in silence, watching. Neither of them stood up for me. The betrayal was suffocating, a weight on my chest that made it hard to breathe.

I nodded, whispering, "Okay." Then, I got up and walked away.

I didn't look back. I got in my car, told my brothers to get in, and drove off. My hands shook on the steering wheel, my vision blurred with tears. No one prepares you for this. No one tells you what to do when your best friends decide they don't need you anymore.

When I got home, I simply told my mom, "I'm not going to youth group anymore."

Because my three girls—my best friends—had made their choice. And it wasn't me.

No one warns you how easily love—the kind you thought would last—can slip through your fingers. Love should come with a warning sign. Caution - some hands you hold will let go.

Even as I grieved that loss, a part of me still held onto the hope that love could look different. In friendships, and in romance. That maybe, somewhere, it was still waiting for me. I've always been a hopeless romantic, searching for my own Prince Charming. I fully blame Disney and High School Musical for raising my expectations, and by high school, I longed for someone to like me, to take me to a dance. I wanted a dancing in the rain moment like Troy and Gabriella, and Prince Naveen? All I can say is I was a child with a juice box and a dream. But by college, having never been in a relationship, I started to wonder if love just wasn't in the cards for me.

At nineteen, I ventured onto dating apps and started talking to a guy a few years older. My family and I now call him "Psychopath"—and for good reason. After chatting for a while, he asked me out, and I nervously agreed. We met at a bowling alley, where I fumbled my way through the game. At some point, knowing I had never kissed anyone, he issued an ultimatum: "If you get a strike, you have to kiss me." Then, "If you get a gutter ball, you have to kiss me." He eventually kissed me, and I was excited—someone actually liked me.

After that, he wanted to hang out every day, but I had three jobs that summer and couldn't keep up with his demands. I also just wanted some time to myself. When I declined a few meet-ups, he called me and told me to quit at least one of my jobs so I could spend more time with him—offering to pay for my missed paychecks, and even college, if I did. I quickly refused. I mean, who offers to fund your unemployment for love? I think he wanted me to swoon, but I kind of wanted to report him. And things only escalated from there.

One night, after I declined another hangout to be with family, he called, cursing me out. He told me I needed to prioritize him over work, family, and even my own introversion. Mind you, he wasn't even my boyfriend yet. I remember standing there, listening to his commands, and for a moment, I almost agreed—just to keep him around. But I realized he was asking me to give up all of me before we even began.

I told him no. He hung up, before proceeding to call me eight more times.

His final message? "If this is how you're going to act, you'll never find someone." It broke me—confirming my biggest fear. I wanted to be loved so badly that, for a moment, sacrificing myself felt worth it. I was willing to bend every boundary just to keep from being alone. But if love meant losing myself to keep them, it was never love to begin with.

After Psychopath and another failed one-date attempt, I had lost all hope. By the middle of my sophomore year, I decided to take a break from dating. But one afternoon, I got a Snapchat follow request from someone I had met a year prior. I'll call him what I did back then—Football Guy. As you can guess, he played football at my college. I liked him when we first met, so I followed him back. I had no idea he'd be the most recent guy I'd let into my heart.

We started talking and spent all of winter break messaging back and forth. By the time we were back on campus, he had already asked to hang out. By our second time together, I felt more comfortable with him than with any guy before. He made me laugh. He made me feel safe. We talked for hours and hours, days passing us by.

Our first official date—a double movie feature—was on my twentieth birthday, and we ended the night with a kiss. Days later, something I had dreamed of since I was a little girl finally happened: I had a boyfriend.

With Football Guy, I experienced so many firsts—the biggest one being love. We met each other's families, visited each other's home states, and fell deeper as the seasons changed. I made outfits for his games, watched him graduate college, exchanged gifts, celebrated an anniversary, and talked about the future. I truly thought he was my future. We always said we'd do life together. I felt so blessed, having found someone who loved me for me.

Then, in March 2023, he had to move away to start a career in football. I was terrified. Long distance had a bad reputation for a reason. But he reassured me, told me I had nothing to worry about, and I believed him. I stole a pillow and one last kiss, and then he drove away.

Things changed, and at first, I ignored the signs. When my mom and I decided to write this book, I texted him excitedly, expecting to celebrate the amazing relationship I was in. But as time passed, the less we talked. I found myself asking for things I never thought I'd have to—more time, more attention, more effort. Suddenly, our relationship felt like an afterthought. He insisted nothing was wrong, but I felt the shift.

By the time he visited Colorado again, I didn't know what I was fighting for anymore. He wouldn't look at me the same way. His effort unraveled in pieces—until he stopped showing up at all. Sometimes he saw me. But when he had a five-hour layover in my city and still didn't want to see me—called it "business," said it wasn't worth the time—it became harder to pretend I was a priority. But I loved him, and he said he was trying. So, I stayed.

Senior year came, and every conversation felt strained. The effort between us was unbalanced, and I felt like I was the only one carrying the weight of us. Eventually I suggested a break, begging him to figure out what he wanted—to fight for me. The last time I saw him, he promised he would.

Three weeks later, he broke up with me.

I still don't understand why. After nearly two years of being loved and fought for, suddenly, it wasn't enough. How could he love me, but not enough to stay? To fight? I thought that if love was real, it wouldn't stop. We had made all these plans for a future that only I showed up for.

To say the heartache has shattered me is an understatement. The first is unlike any other. I'm mourning someone who's still alive, carrying love for a person who seems to have thrown it away. I thought I'd write this chapter excited, happy, but instead, what I thought was forever turned into just another lesson.

For who? I don't know.

Love has been taken—time and time again. But I've also seen the many ways God has brought love into my life in ways I never would've dreamed of, even the love that left scars. If I could love the wrong person—people—that deeply, only God knows how much I'll love the one who's meant for me.

"It is not the job of the child to protect her mother. It's the mother's job to protect the child. By allowing your mother to protect you, you gave her a gift."
- Kristin Cashore

CHAPTER SEVEN

Loss

Olivia's Perspective

Grief is not just an emotion—it's an unraveling. It is an empty seat at the table, a space where something once lived but is now gone. It carves through you, leaving a hollow ache where love once resided.

In the beginning, it's unbearable, like a wound that will never close. You wake up and forget, just for a second, that they're gone. And then it hits you, like a crash of waves that refuses to relent. But over time, the raw edges begin to mend—not because the loss gets smaller, but because you learn how to carry it. The pain softens, but the imprint remains—a quiet reminder of what once was. The truth is, you never truly "move on." You move *with* it. The love you had does not disappear; it transforms. It lingers in the echoes of laughter, in the warmth of old memories, in the silent moments where you still reach for what is no longer there.

And that's okay.

Grief is not a burden to be hidden. It is not a weakness to be ashamed of. It is the deepest proof that love existed, that something beautiful once touched your life. So let yourself feel it. Let yourself mourn. Let yourself remember.

There is no timeline, no "right" way to grieve. Some days will be heavy, and some will feel lighter. Some moments will bring unexpected waves of sadness, while others will fill you with gratitude for the love you were lucky enough to experience.

As hard as it is, I'm slowly learning to honor my grief, for it is sacred. It is a testament to the depth of my heart. And in time, through the pain, I will find healing—not because I have forgotten, but because I have learned how to carry both love and loss together.

2020 and 2021 took everything out of me. They brought loss after loss. It was like being trapped in a relentless storm, each wave knocking me down before I could catch my breath. I had spent years perfecting the art of keeping it together—smiling through pain, showing up when I wanted to shut down—but nothing could prepare me for this. First my dad. Then my close friend. Then my bonus dad. Back-to-back. No time to process, no time to breathe.

First, my dad. Then, just when I thought I had no tears left to cry, I lost a close friend—suddenly, out of the blue.

I couldn't even put words to how much she meant to me, how deeply she had influenced my life. And yet, even after she was gone, she continued to inspire me, still challenged me, still made me pause and reflect on the work I was doing and the lives I was impacting.

I found myself looking back at her handwritten goals from the first edition of my book—words she had poured into me over eight years ago. And in the quiet moments, I could still hear her voice, clear as day, saying, *Liv, you got this!*

Then, not long after, my bonus dad—after a long several years of sickness and hospitalizations.

To have more than one father is a blessing I never could have anticipated, but for 25 years, he never treated me as anything less than his daughter. I had already buried one father, and now, I had to say goodbye to another. Seeing yet another loved one leave this earth felt unbearable. But the peace, the joy, the wholeness I knew he was experiencing on the other side—that brought me some comfort.

But no matter how much I tried to hold onto that peace, the weight of the losses crushed me. One after another, grief kept knocking at my door, and I had no choice but to let it in.

Losing my father and the way he left was so unexpected in so many unexpected ways.

I sent him a text on Valentine's Day that simply said, "I love you."

That was it. No long message, no over-explaining. Just those three words.

Sending any type of communication to him was a risk. Over the years, I had learned that reaching out could be met with resentment, a sharp reminder of the distance between us.

"Wow, I didn't expect to hear from you."
"Wow, you finally reached out."

Every time, it sent the abandoned little girl in me into a tailspin. *You're the parent. The phone rings both ways. You can reach out.*

So, my expectations were low when I sent this particular text. I didn't need a conversation. I just wanted him to know that I truly loved him.

His response came almost immediately.

"What a surprise! Thank you, my darling daughter. I am very proud of you. I love you very much. Happy Valentine's Day!"

It was thoughtful. Kind. Softer than usual. And I had no idea those would be the last words he would tell me.

I love yous weren't common in my family. They weren't casually spoken or easily given. I had spent years saying those words and getting nothing in return, a silence that used to sting but had slowly turned into something I had learned to expect.

Two weeks later, he was gone.

Losing a parent to suicide creates a grief that is unlike any other. It is complicated, filled with questions that have no answers. *What if I had called instead of texted? What if I had said something different? What if, what if, what if...*

It wouldn't have mattered. Fourteen days later, it would have been too late.

The emotions hit like a wrecking ball—devastation, anger, sadness, frustration, guilt, regret. They don't come in phases. They don't follow an order. They cycle, over and over, just when you think you've caught your breath. The minute I think I've found a silver lining or a bright side, it gets swept away by darkness.

But in the midst of that darkness, I have found one small truth to hold onto:

This was not about me.

My dad didn't leave because of me. His love for me did not die with him. His pain was bigger than I will ever understand, and it was never a reflection of my worth or my love for him.

I remind myself of this over and over, on the days when the guilt creeps in.

And I remind myself that grief is love's final act.

It hurts this much because it meant something. Because it still means something. And that will never change.

There were many late-night and early-morning conversations with God where I felt like I could get a glimpse into my dad's complex mind and shattered heart. I would lie awake, staring at the ceiling, trying to piece together the fragments of his pain, searching for clues in the memories I had left. Some nights, I begged God to help me understand. Other nights, I sat in silence, waiting for an answer that never came.

I had to remind myself frequently—*obsessively*—that when someone chooses to leave this earth, it is not a direct reflection of the
amount of love they had for you. Or the love you had for them.

But that reminder didn't always stick.

The following years would bring more losses. People I loved—
gone, one after another. I felt like life was slipping through my fingers at every turn. On any given week or month, there was news of
someone else. Another person was taken. Another name added to
the ever-growing list of people I would never see again.

Just a couple weeks after my dad's death, the entire world would
shut down overnight.

The pandemic forced us inside, left us alone with our grief,
made us sit in it, stare at it, *face it*—head-on. There were no distractions, no escape. We weren't allowed to be busy. We weren't allowed
to run.

So, like most people, I found ways to prepare.

I went to the grocery store and stocked up on non-perishable
food, making sure I had enough to feed the house for at least a couple of weeks. And like many others, I stopped by the liquor store.

It felt like we were preparing for a blizzard—the kind where the
power might go out, but you make the best of it anyway. You stock
up on snacks, blankets, and board games. You make it a fun little
vacation. You hunker down with movies, warm drinks, and whatever
will get you through.

At first, that's what it felt like.

I became a bit of a bartender, experimenting with cocktails, making the best of an impossible situation. I told myself it was fine. That we were all just coping.

But a few months later, when the lockdown lifted, and we were faced with a "new normal" my drinking didn't stop.

I justified it.

I had just lost my dad, among all things. After a long day of work, a glass of wine was my reward. During a rough night when sleep wouldn't come, a glass of wine was my comfort. And when I would wake at four in the morning, haunted by nightmares, a glass of wine would calm me.

Even on good days—when I landed a new piece of business, helped someone launch a big project, or finally went a full day without crying—I gave myself a reward: a glass of wine.

Or two.

I was aware. Painfully aware.

And according to society's standards, one glass a day—even two glasses—wasn't that big of a deal. It was normal. Acceptable. Encouraged, even.

But I knew me.

And I knew this was not me.

What started as a glass turned into a bottle. What started as an occasional comfort turned into a crutch.

And then, one morning, I woke up and simply said, *enough is enough*.

I made the choice, and I stopped. I started to make efforts to examine my intentions, to ask myself why—why I was reaching for it, why I thought I needed it, why I was numbing instead of healing.

And then, I faced the real work: learning how to sit with the pain instead of silencing it.

Music has always been a time machine for me—a portal to comfort, joy, and heart-wrenching pain. Certain songs carry entire memories within them, embedding themselves into the fabric of who we are.

After my dad passed, I couldn't listen to the songs he loved without breaking down. It was as if each lyric, each familiar melody, carried the weight of his absence.

One afternoon, I was driving home from the grocery store, masked up, adjusting to a world that never really felt normal again. And then, *Yearning for Your Love* by The Gap Band came on the radio.

I froze. My hands gripped the steering wheel. My chest tightened and the tears came like a flood.

It had only been a few days since he decided to leave, and yet the pain felt centuries old. Even now, when that song plays, I have to brace myself—forcing back the tears, longing for a day when I can hear it and feel something other than loss. A day when I can sing along out of gratitude and joy for the good things he brought to this world.

Because there *were* good things.

I learned, after he was no longer here, about the man he had been before me. The people he impacted. The communities he saved. The legacy he left—all before I was even born.

This was a different man.

The father I wished I had... was a father to so many others.

It's strange, the way grief shifts over time. At first, all I could see was what I lost. But as the years passed, I began to find something else—a different kind of love for him. Not just as my father, but as a human being, flawed and fragile, yet capable of so much. It gave me a new sense of pride in being his daughter, an urgency to create, build, record, and write—to leave my own legacy.

Because time is short. And precious.

Every year, as the anniversary of his death approached, I could feel it creeping in—the uneasiness, the tension, the subtle yet forceful reminder that the day was close. My body would remember before my mind did. The exhaustion, the heavy sadness pressing against my chest, the way I would snap at small things without realizing why.

So, I started taking the day off work every year.

Not so much to *honor* him, but to protect and honor *myself*.

To give myself space. To grieve on my own terms. To let whatever emotions that surfaced have their moment before I had to tuck them back away again.

And then, a year and a half later, the weight of grief doubled. Quadrupled really.

My little sister took her life.

On our dad's birthday.

The air was sucked out of me when I heard the news. I knew she missed him. She had told me before that he was the only one who really *got* her. But I never imagined... not like this.

She had been diagnosed with bipolar disorder many years ago, and more recently, borderline personality disorder. I noticed shifts in her throughout high school, but nothing that couldn't be brushed off as typical teenage emotions. Then, in college, another shift—one that never quite settled.

For almost ten years, it felt like we were slowly losing her.

And then, suddenly, all at once.

This loss didn't make sense.

When we lost my grandma—my mom's mom—it was unbearably hard especially for her. I can't imagine the hole that losing a mother leaves behind. I was out of town when I got the call super early in the morning.

When my phone rang and it was my mom I had a feeling about what happened. I was so far away and couldn't be there for her or Malia like I wanted to and like I'm sure they needed. Even though she had lived 97 full years, it still hit all of us like a wave I wasn't prepared for. But in some way, I could accept it. It made *sense*.

When my other grandma—my dad's mom—passed on, she had been suffering from the debilitating side effects of Alzheimer's. That was also hard, but again, it *made sense*.

But this? This wasn't fair.

I turned the blame inward. I questioned everything. What could I have done differently?

What if I had called her more? What if I had pushed her harder to get the help she needed? What if I had been enough to keep her here?

But the truth—the devastating, gut-wrenching truth—is that you can love someone with everything you have, but if they don't want to be here, there is nothing you can say or do to stop them.

And yet, even knowing that, my anger still found a target.

I blamed my dad.

Maybe if he hadn't made such a selfish decision, she would still be here. Maybe if he had *stayed*, she wouldn't have followed.

I know that's my grief talking.

I know that when I step back, when I let the anger settle, I can see the layers of it all—the weight of their pain, the depths of their suffering, the illnesses they carried that were bigger than love could heal.

But knowing doesn't make it easier.

I feel like I was right there—taking her to and from appointments, sitting with her at the grocery store, trying to pull her out of seclusion, listening as she unraveled her thoughts, desperately trying to make sense of the world.

She had a beautiful smile—one that she used to hide her pain more often than not. She had a laugh that, when genuine, could light up a room.

She lived for her boys.
She loved her boys.

And for that, I'm proud of her.

I know that the immense grief I feel is only a *fraction* of the peace she has now found.

And maybe that's the hardest part. Knowing she's finally free from the pain that tethered her here, but still wishing she had stayed.

Grief doesn't come in neat, manageable waves. It crashes, unexpectedly, and takes you under. Just when you think you've surfaced, that you've found a way to breathe again, another wave pulls you back into the depths.

Losing my sister unearthed my grief for my dad all over again. When I was in the thick of it, drowning in sadness and frustration, reason didn't matter. Logic didn't help. It was easier to place blame than to sit with the unbearable truth—that loss can be layered, tangled, and impossible to make sense of.

It took me years, but I'm slowly learning how to grieve better, healthier.

Grief in and of itself isn't bad.

It doesn't go away. But if you let it, it evolves. And if you allow it, it can even become beautiful.

Looking back, I regret that my way of coping was to act like everything was fine—especially for my kids.

It was like those times when your toddler is first learning to walk, wobbling on unsteady legs before inevitably taking a dive. As a parent, you have a choice in how you react.

You can pretend you didn't see them fall, hoping to lessen their reaction. Or you can acknowledge it, keep your cool, and make it seem like no big deal—again, trying to minimize their response.

That was how I handled death.

I told my kids about each loss matter-of-factly, nonchalantly, with little emotion. Then, I'd immediately follow it up with a silver-lining statement. *They're in a better place now. Everything will be okay.* I also tried to keep it a little hush hush how they died. I didn't want them to feel or carry the weight of it. So I omitted that little detail when sharing the news. I was such an idiot.

I went about life like I hadn't just dropped a bomb on them.

But they weren't toddlers learning to walk.

They were teenagers who needed an example of what healthy grieving looked like.

They needed to see me cry.

To see me in pain.
To see me miss them.
To hear me recount stories.

They needed to see me singing along to the songs that re-minded me of my dad and my sister. And to see me break down, and then laugh, and then rebuild.

But instead, just like I had done with the disco balls and the dance parties—the joyful distractions I created in the wake of my divorce—I convinced myself that if they thought I was okay, then they would be okay.

But what they needed was my realness.

I did the same thing in my dysfunctional, abusive marriage—and again, as it unraveled into divorce.

I held everything together like I was the glue, the one who had to keep things from shattering. And so, I acted like I was fine. Like everything was under control.

By that point, my kids weren't babies. They weren't small chil-dren. They were practically young adults.

So, when everything came to a head, and I finally threw my things into boxes and told my son, Pack your things. We are leaving in the morning, I will never forget the look of shock on his face.

Because he didn't know how bad it was.

He didn't know we had reached a place where I literally needed to flee, to start over completely.

I know now that this is no way to prepare your kids for the real world.

But I also know that as they watch me now—see me beginning to adopt healthier concepts of grief, see me learning how to sit with loss instead of running from it, see me finding more expressive, true coping mechanisms—they can model the good, the real things.

And together, we can be there for each other—every step of the way.

Malia's Perspective

Heaven was a concept I learned young. I imagined it as peaceful and beautiful—though the "beautiful" part came from *Hercules* and not theology. Sunday School taught me it was a place without sadness, pain, or fear, where we'd be with Jesus forever. My dad's church had a song that described it as a "big, big house with lots of food and football." But Heaven is up there, and I am down here. It was comforting to think about, but only when everyone I loved was still here with me.

At my charter school, music class was a highlight. Whether it was getting on the bleachers, playing musical chairs, or playing with instruments, we got to create beautiful sounds. Our music teacher had an infectious passion for music and an even greater love for us. Whether working with kindergartners or fifth graders, she brought out something special in each of us. Her biggest productions were the Winter Concert and the Talent Show, and in middle school, she introduced my class to Shakespeare. I grew in my stage presence and confidence, performing at Denver's Annual Shakespeare Festival multiple times with her support. She helped me discover the joy of music and self-expression, and her love never wavered.

Then, at the start of seventh grade, we got the news—our music teacher had ovarian cancer. My homeroom teacher's words stunned us into silence. We all knew what cancer was; some of us knew it too well. But she was hopeful. School continued, and so did she. We sang, we played instruments. But soon enough, we started to get substitutes. When our teacher did show up, her smile was smaller. On occasion, her hair would swish in a way it had never done before. Things slowly started to change, but her light never dimmed.

February 2016 brought an epic snowstorm, giving us two snow days in a row. The days were earned too, as it had snowed so badly that it nearly covered cars. I had woken up the first morning, excited for breakfast and getting to read all day long. I had picked up my phone to check my messages, and there was only one that mattered. One of my friends had blown up our group chat.

"Our music teacher is dead."

No soft phrasing—just *dead*. I dropped my phone, my mind unable to grasp it. I told my family, but none of us understood. Yes, she had cancer, but what did this mean? My parents told us she was in Heaven, but did that mean we'd never see her smile again? No more concerts? No more encouragement? The light I never thought would dim had gone out.

Back at school, counselors were available, but I didn't go. I thought I understood—cancer won. But I couldn't wrap my head around never seeing her again. The hallways sounded different. Music class wasn't the same.

A few weeks later, we held a ceremony for our music teacher. It coincided with Literacy Day, an event I had started at my school. I was asked to both sing in her honor with other students and give my annual Literacy Day speech. When I spoke, I cried. I didn't want to talk about the joy of reading when our joy of music was missing.

I couldn't understand where we stood as individuals—or where we, as a school, were headed next. After my speech, more words were said before we all moved outside to release teal balloons, the color that represents ovarian cancer. As we released the balloons into the sky, Heaven didn't feel like a fun, peaceful place anymore. It felt like a place that took my love away.

Losing my music teacher was the first time I felt the weight of grief pressing down on me, the first time I realized that love doesn't stop loss from coming.

In 2018, another loss knocked closer to home. My great-grandma, an incredible fighter, had always bounced back from hardships. Every fall, every accident—she always recovered. Around my family and some friends, I would describe her as an awesome, powerful bouncy ball. I told them, as I tell them now, my great-grandma always bounced back. What I never thought I'd witness, at least for a long time, was the day that she wouldn't.

She had a bad fall at the end of 2017. And this time, it felt different. My mom and grandma were more worried than usual. But I had no doubt; I truly believed she would recover. She always did.

As a child, I thought it was amazing that she was nearing 100 years old. It felt like an achievement. But as I got older, and saw my great-grandma move slower, I realized how long and heavy a century could be.

In May of 2018, Grandma T was moved to hospice care—a term I naively understood as just another hospital. I went to youth group, and one night during prayer requests, I asked for healing—for God to take all her pain away. Later that night, I stayed at my grandma's house, and I didn't know prayers could be answered in ways I never expected. God heard me, but not in the way I had intended.

At midnight, I woke up to my grandma standing in the dark, unnervingly calm. "I got a call from hospice," she said. "It's Grandma T. There isn't much time."

None of it made sense. I fumbled for my phone and shoes, grabbed a blanket, and rushed out the door. The car ride was suffocatingly silent, and it was then that I realized I had never done this before. The car needed advice, support, maybe even laughter, but I looked to my grandma for those things. I was at a loss for words on how to provide that. I wanted my mom.

The hospice center was eerily quiet. A few doctors lingered, some lights were off. We walked down the hallways to Grandma T's room. She lay tucked under hospital blankets, in a medically induced coma. The pain was finally too much. We settled in, waiting, though I didn't know what for.

Her breathing was slow and soft. The room felt frozen in time. Our pastors arrived, and dread settled in. If Grandma T was going to pull through, they didn't need to be here. One of them told me to talk to her, to say what I needed to say. But how do you say goodbye when it doesn't feel real?

At some point, my grandma and the pastors stepped out. I moved closer to Grandma T, memorizing her face, imagining her smile. I whispered memories—of our visits, of the honey jar she kept filled with Cheerios.

"I love you," I said. Then, after a pause, tears finally forming, I whispered, "It's okay. You can go."

The night blurred after that. I dozed off in the recliner, exhausted. I opened my eyes again when Grandma T took her final breath. The room, impossibly, grew even quieter. A doctor entered, speaking softly with my grandma. I couldn't hear them. I held her hand one last time before we left the room.

Grandma didn't say anything, and I wouldn't know what to say back. What do you say to a daughter who has lost their mother?

Nothing felt real. I was weightless, unanchored, drifting through a world that no longer made sense. My grandma and I reached the hospice entrance, passing a lounge area with a Keurig. We lingered, then quietly made ourselves cups of hot chocolate. At 4 a.m., it was the best hot chocolate I'd ever had. We smiled, even giggled, at the simple goodness in our hands. It wasn't anything special—just water and cocoa—but it filled the hollow space starting to form in our hearts.

Watching a loved one pass is unlike anything I've ever experienced. Time is never enough, and love holds on even as they slip away. I had prayed for healing, and God answered in His way—by bringing my great-grandma to Heaven, letting her rest at last. She was finally at peace, but I was not. Heaven felt too far away.

Grief, I was coming to understand, doesn't get easier with time—it just gets more familiar. My mom's dad wasn't around much. He rarely visited, and when he did, the visits were always... interesting, to say the least. He was well-trained in martial arts and would show us some moves, his hands steady and precise, his presence always a little larger than life.

There's a photo of him that has always been one of my favorites. In it, he's holding my hand and my brother's—one of us on each side. He's wearing what I had always seen him in: a hat and a suit, looking as if he had just stepped out of another era. I, on the other hand, am in the cutest pink ballerina outfit, my hair styled in two neat buns, my tiny dance tote slung over my shoulder. My brother, still small, is in an orange sweatshirt. I guess he must have been taking me to dance class, the one just across the street from the house.

Beyond that image, he was hard to pin down. The little I knew came from my mom, and even then, the picture was incomplete. She didn't talk about him much, but when she did, it was clear that their relationship was complicated—far more layered than I could fully grasp. He was, in many ways, a mystery. Beyond the fact that he was the start of my family—bringing my mom, aunts, and uncles into the world—and the fact that he wasn't always there for my mom, there wasn't much else I needed to know. He was just my grandfather.

When I was told he had passed away, my heart sank. A strange, heavy grief settled in, but I wasn't sure where it was rooted. We weren't close. But he was my mom's father. I knew that she had lost someone—someone who had shaped her life in ways both visible and invisible. Watching her process his death made everything feel even more complex, and I couldn't begin to imagine what she was feeling.

A few days, maybe weeks, later, my mom finally told me what happened.

He had taken his own life.

The news hit like a punch to the gut. My shock and sadness begged for someplace to land, but I didn't know where to put them. The sadness came not just from the loss itself but from the way it had happened—from the weight of a choice I couldn't begin to understand.

It left me wanting to know him more, to understand him in a way I never had the chance to. I wanted to know his story—not just the fragments passed down in quiet conversations, but the full picture. I wanted to understand the loss I was grieving. But I couldn't. And maybe I never will.

If I ever see him again—if there is a moment beyond this life where we cross paths—I don't even know what I would say. Maybe I'd ask him about that photo, about that day when he walked me to dance class. Maybe I'd ask him to teach me some of those martial arts moves he used to show us. Or maybe I wouldn't ask him anything at all. Maybe I would just sit with him, existing in whatever space eternity allows, and finally know him in a way I never did before. Maybe that will be enough.

Losing my grandpa left a hole that couldn't be filled, only carried. I thought I understood grief by then, how it works, how it lingers. But grief doesn't play by rules, and it doesn't wait for you to be ready.

I had a family friend that I met when I was young, and calling him a ball of energy would be an understatement. He was full of light, making every moment chaotic fun. Our families had a blast whenever we were together, and it never felt like anything else. The day my dad told me he was sick, I felt a bittersweet mix of fear and certainty. God knew what was happening, and He would fix it. He always had—why wouldn't He now?

But the sickness became cancer, and I couldn't understand. He wasn't supposed to get worse; it was supposed to go away. He was just a kid, my brother's age. Our parents urged us to pray, so I did, and I told others to as well. My frustration faded because I trusted God would heal him.

Then, during the holidays, my dad gathered us at the table. The only times we sat down like that were when something was seriously wrong. My dad, usually clear-spoken, struggled for words. When he finally said our friend wasn't going to get better, my body went numb. My youngest brother smiled, asking when he would recover if not now. My stepbrother, who knew him best, had nothing to say, just tears on his face. My brother closest in age stood up and walked away, anger and frustration masking his sadness. All I could do was hold my tears and pick at the tablemats, lost and confused.

Right after Christmas, our families spent a weekend in the mountains together. Our friend couldn't move much, but he was still with us. He taught me a new game, played music he liked, and told me where my brothers were hiding during a game of hide-and-seek. We all got matching pajamas, watched movies, and soaked in the warming moments. That snowy weekend became one of our last together.

February brought bitter cold and worsening news. Every phone call made my stomach drop. Even my school counselor, a kind Christian man, checked in on me weekly, though I didn't know what to say. Then, late one afternoon, we drove down a snowy street, among the first families to be invited to say goodbye. My dad's hands tensed on the steering wheel, his eyes searching for answers he couldn't give us. I had never known my dad not to have an answer, and I wasn't sure what scared me more—that he didn't know, or that he knew but couldn't tell me.

Our friend was asleep when we arrived, but when he woke, he recognized each of us by name. We talked about school, sports, and the weather, pretending it was just another visit. As we left, I touched his hand and made one last desperate plea. *Please, God. I beg of You.*

"Bye," I said, smiling as much joy as I could put into those words. He didn't respond, but he smiled back. That was enough.

Two weeks later, my dad called. Our friend had passed peacefully, at home, in his mother's arms.

I told my mom I was going to get food, though I don't know why she let me drive. Tears blurred my vision as I tried to escape, but you can't drive away from heartache. Back home, I tore apart my bed, needing to do something, anything. Then I collapsed onto my knees, bruising them on the floor. I sat with my anger long enough to finally realize it was grief. I couldn't understand. God should have saved His child. It wasn't fair.

The end of May brought our friend's memorial service, high in the mountains where he loved to be. I felt numb the whole drive up. Surrounded by his family, classmates, and others, we listened to stories of his kindness, bravery, and hope. But as much as I knew he was at peace, down here, it was the complete opposite.

Then, the time came to spread his ashes. Each of us could take a small scoop and scatter it across the mountain. I stayed back, unwilling to accept it, unwilling to move forward. My dad gently rubbed my back. "You should get in line, Malia," he said. "I don't want to. I can't," I replied.

"If you leave here without saying goodbye, you'll regret it," he said, pulling me into a hug. It took several more seconds, but I finally stepped into line. Now, I have to remember someone longer than I knew them.

By now, loss felt like an unwelcome visitor I couldn't keep out. Each time, I hoped it would be the last—that the people I loved would stay. But hope didn't stop the phone call I never wanted to get. This time, it was different. This time, the loss wasn't just painful—it was full of questions I would never get answers to.

My aunt was one of the kindest people I knew. She was sweet, bubbly, and always had something interesting to say, her laughter unmistakable—light and full, like a melody only she could create. I got to know her more as I grew up, mostly at family gatherings, where she made every conversation feel warm and full of life.

Her first son was one of the first cousins I truly got to know. I still remember meeting them both for the first time when my mom, brother, and I drove up into the mountains to visit. As I got older, through high school and into graduation, I grew even closer to her, watching as she built her family. At one point, she moved in with my grandmother, and I saw her more often, our relationship shifting into something more personal.

Spending time with her was always memorable—sometimes fun, sometimes different. She had her struggles, and as I got older, I became more aware of how much she needed support. Many of my later memories with her involved helping her in some way, whether it was moving her into a new home or helping her make lasagna for friends. Sometimes, it was simply being there when she needed someone. Most of the time, she was happy, her joy filling the spaces around her. But other times, she seemed weighed down, her emotions shifting more often, the light in her eyes dimming.

In the months before I left for college, she began pulling away. I didn't see her as much, and when I did, I was told not to ask questions—just to be there for her, to remind her that I loved her. I didn't fully understand what was happening, but I followed what I was told. The last time I saw her, she was quiet. But I hugged her tight and told her I loved her, hoping those words reached her in the way I meant them to.

Then, right before Thanksgiving, my mom called. Her voice was urgent, asking if I was alone. When she learned I was, she told me to find a friend to be with me. And then, when I did, she told me.

My aunt was gone.

I started crying immediately, the grief crashing over me like a wave I wasn't ready for. What else was there to do but cry? Why? My mom, holding back her own tears, stayed on the phone with me, but I couldn't process the weight of it. I didn't want to lose anyone else. I had already lost too much. After a moment, I wiped my face and went to work, hoping—foolishly—that I could outrun the sorrow.

A few mornings later, I saw my mom's post on Instagram. And that was how I found out.

She had taken her own life.

I was sitting in church when I read it, and suddenly, I felt frozen. I couldn't break down here. I couldn't cry like I wanted to. But my mind was racing. Not again. Not this way.

My last moments with her replayed in my head. Had I told her I loved her? I had. But did she know how much? Did she understand how deeply we all cared? Guilt settled in, twisting into confusion and anger.

What had we missed?

What had I missed?

Had our love not been enough?

I was mad at everything—the situation, the weight of it all. I was mad at my mom for not telling me in person. But then I thought of her own grief, her own pain in losing a sister, in trying to make sense of something that would never have a clear answer.

If I could see my aunt again, I don't know if I would even speak. I think I would just hold her, the way I wish she had needed to be held in this life. A hug that maybe would've been enough.

It took me a long time to process her loss—the loss of the others I had loved—my grandfather, my great-grandmother, my teacher, and my friend. That pain never truly goes away. But I've come to realize I don't want it to. Because if the grief is still there, it means the love hasn't faded.

Before my aunt's memorial, my mom and some of my other aunts got a butterfly tattoo in her honor. I wasn't ready then. I wanted more time to sit with my memories of her, of my grandfather, of my great-grandmother—to understand what they meant to me.

And so, in August of 2023, I honored them in my own way. I got a tattoo of flowers, with my aunt's butterfly nestled among them, carrying them with me on the journey they could no longer walk.

I hope, wherever they are, it is a place full of peace. A place where they are finally held the way they always deserved to be.

"With the help of God, [my daughter is]
the best thing I have ever been a part of."
- Serena Williams

CHAPTER EIGHT

Faith

Olivia's Perspective

Faith looks like taking your power back when you've been running on empty for what felt like decades. It looks like deciding that enough is enough—filing for divorce not because you stopped loving someone, but because you finally started loving yourself. It looks like packing up your life, moving to a new city with nothing but prayer and a list of scriptures full of hope. It looks like enrolling in grad school while navigating grief, bills, brain fog, deadlines, and fighting for your life against perimenopause—the uninvited guest that crashes into your hormones like a drunk driver at a red light.

It looks like writing a whole book in the middle of that storm. Choosing to tell your story while still living it. Not because everything is resolved or picture-perfect, but because you know there's power in telling the truth while it's still raw.

Faith is doing all of that all together.

I mean, I didn't die. So, there's that.

And I say that with both sarcasm and sincerity. There were moments—deep in the middle of it—when I wasn't sure I would make it. When my racing mind and anxiety-filled chest couldn't seem to hold off the panic attacks. When the weight of everything felt too heavy, too layered, too relentless. But I woke up the next day. And the next one. And each time, I kept going. That, in itself, is faith.

When people talk about faith, they often quote Hebrews 11:1: "Faith shows the reality of what we hope for; it is the evidence of things we cannot see." And while I understand and believe in the power of that verse, let me just be real—it sounds poetic and powerful, sure. But also? A little confusing. Churchy. The kind of scripture that makes you go, "Yes, Lord!" in the moment... and then Google it later to figure out what it actually means and its practical application to my real, messy life.

So, let's break it down in plain, teenager-like terms. Because I've been a teenager. I've raised teenagers. And I've led many sermons and Bible studies for teenagers who pretended to understand something just to avoid being called on to read aloud.

Faith is like having this strong, illogical, borderline unreasonable belief in something you can't see or prove, but you know deep in your soul is real. Like a secret you're absolutely sure is true even though no one else knows it. Like remembering a cool thing that happened at a party even though you forgot to take a picture for social media. And since you didn't post it, people might question it. But you know what happened. You felt it. That's faith.

Or to put it another way, as the wonderful Patrick Swayze once sang: "She's like the wind."

The *Dirty Dancing* soundtrack isn't just iconic—it's unexpectedly spiritual. We can't see the wind, but we know it's there. We feel it. It shifts the trees, it whips our hair (well not my hair), it slams car doors shut before we're ready. Wind is invisible and undeniable at the same time.

It moves. It shifts. It carries. And sometimes, it shows up when you least expect it—just in time to keep you from falling apart.

Here's the thing: faith doesn't require proof. It just requires presence. A willingness to show up with your doubts and your fear and your trembling hands and say, "God, I'm here. I don't know how this is going to work out, but I'm trusting that You do."

The story of my life.

Faith simply means believing that something is true—and then taking action based on that belief. And this is the part where I've often struggled.

Because I'm great at the believing part. Oh, I can believe all day. I've got journals full of scriptures, promises, prophecies, and prayers. I've got vision boards. I've got devotionals with highlighted pages and worn-out covers. I've even got faith merch! I've got the T-shirts that say "Faith Over Fear" and mugs that exclaim "God's Got This."

But the action part? That's harder.

Because sometimes I believe God will handle something, so I step back and do nothing—convincing myself that waiting is the same thing as trusting. That passivity is actually patience. But sometimes that's not true faith. That's what I call *safe faith*.

The kind that stays on the shore when you're being called to walk on water. I never really technically learned to swim so this is me all day.

The kind that looks like surrender but is really just avoidance.

Again, me.

The kind that says, "God, I trust You... as long as You don't ask me to change anything or be uncomfortable."

Safe faith protects us from disappointment. But it also protects us from miracles. It keeps us from stepping into the unknown—and into the very blessing we've been praying for.

And I have lived in that "safe faith" zone more times than I'd like to admit. Not in every area of my life—but definitely in the areas where the stakes felt highest. The places where I was the most tender. The dreams I wanted most but was too afraid to pursue, because what if I leapt and fell? What if I hoped—and God didn't come through?

That kind of fear is real. And it doesn't just come out of nowhere.

At one point, I had to sit myself down and name something I didn't want to face: that my limited faith had more to do with my wounds than my spirituality. That my hesitation wasn't about whether God was capable. He can do anything. It was more about whether I could trust that He would…for me.

Because here's the truth: I had been hurt by promises before.

My dad, though full of good intentions in his own way, was a big promise guy. Huge declarations. Grandiose plans. He'd look you in the eyes, swear on everything, and make you feel like the world was yours. And then, more often than not, those promises would fall through. Sometimes it was circumstances or lack of resources. Sometimes it was straight-up avoidance. Whatever the reason, the end result was always the same—a deep disappointment. A trust and expectations that slowly eroded. A feeling that promises were made to be broken.

So, when I first heard "trust the Father," my heart couldn't help but ask, *which one?*

Because the word "Father" carried weight. It came with baggage. It came with the sound of car doors never showing up in the driveway. With the echo of "I'll be there" turning into silence. With the sudden disappearing act on Christmas morning. With the lesson that maybe I should just do things myself so I don't have to feel that kind of letdown again.

But thank God—literally—that I learned to separate the two.

Recognizing that my earthly father, as human and flawed and well-meaning as he may have been, was not the blueprint for God helped me breathe and trust again. It helped me reimagine what it meant to be fathered well. It helped me believe that there is a love that cannot lie. A promise that cannot be broken. A presence that will never disappear.

Trust me, I'm still working on this. And I need reminders every single day.

My Heavenly Father is not a man. He is not bound by time or trauma, mental illness or limitation. He is not flaky. He does not forget. He doesn't show up late, cancel last minute, or ghost me when things get hard. He is faithful. He is constant. He is the only one who cannot fail me.

And slowly, I am letting that truth rewrite the narrative.

I'm still letting it rewrite me.

Because faith is a journey. It's not a one-time altar call or a single mountaintop moment. It's daily. It's choosing to believe again and again—especially when it would be easier not to. It's trusting even when things look blurry and unpromising. It's doing the next right thing even when you're scared. And on some days, it's just getting out of bed and whispering, *God, I trust You today,* even when your circumstances say otherwise.

It's not linear. It's layered.

And it's still unfolding.

Growing up, the religion in our house wasn't Christianity as most people know it. It wasn't Christianity at all.

It was something my dad had... crafted. Pieced together, stitched from various doctrines, Eastern philosophies, and martial arts ideologies, then tied together with his own beliefs and bound by a conviction that he alone had the truth. It was intense. And it placed him—flawed and fully human—at the center of salvation.

There were no children's Bible stories in my childhood. No Veggie Tales. No Sunday school crafts. Our understanding of Jesus was mostly what we saw on TV once a year during Christmas and Easter: the nativity, the baby in the manger, the wise men, then the crucifixion, the cross, and the stone being rolled away. We didn't know much beyond those fleeting scenes. Church wasn't something we did. Jesus wasn't someone we knew.

But one day, a neighbor asked if we wanted to go.

Now, you have to understand—we were homeschooled. And not "co-op, enrichment field trips, online resources" home-schooled. We were 80s homeschooled-homeschooled. As in, left at home. So being invited anywhere felt like a break from solitary con-finement, a golden ticket to freedom. We jumped at the chance.

Looking back, I don't know if it was the sermons, the music, or just the energy of being around other people who didn't share our last name—but that first church began to shift something in me.

In us.

Friendships were formed. Laughter was shared. Scripture started to make its way into our vocabulary—not because someone was drilling it into us, but because it was coming alive in the people around us.

Eventually, my mom started coming, too.

She'd sit in the back at first. Quiet. Reserved. A little unsure. But over time, the walls began to come down. She started building relationships herself, however surface-level they may have felt in the beginning. And slowly, what started as something to do on a boring Sunday or Wednesday night turned into a spiritual spark.

Funny how God works. One invitation, extended in kindness, became a divine seed planted. That seemingly casual moment laid the groundwork for everything that would follow—for me, for my mom, and eventually, for my children. It marked the beginning of a generational shift.

My kids would grow up with a very different experience. They would really know church. They would know Jesus. They would know what it meant to be covered, guided, and loved—not just by us, their parents, but by a whole community of believers.

For a brief season, they were what people call "PKs"—pastor's kids. And yes, the term gets a bad rap. But for them, it was a blessing.

Their dad and I served as youth pastors at a small church where nearly half the congregation was under the age of 18. So from the moment Malia and her brother were born, they were immersed in it. Long Sundays, youth nights, altar calls, potlucks, and church picnics—this was their norm.

That church—*My Father's House*—wasn't just a building. It wasn't even just a place of worship. It was *home*.

It was where they were dedicated. Where they made friends. Where they fell asleep on padded pews and danced and clapped during praise breaks. It was where they heard their names called in prayer, where people they didn't even know were interceding on their behalf.

Malia doesn't remember a single moment in her life without My Father's House. Without the people. The pastors. The music. The love. The Holy Spirit. It's woven into her DNA.

And for me, it was the space where I became a worshiper. Not just someone who sang along as the choir sang—but someone who gave herself over to worship completely. Who wept at the altar. Who danced even when the tears hadn't dried. Who learned to praise in the middle of heartbreak. Who learned that worship wasn't about perfection or performance—but about posture.

Worship became my lifeline. My place to unravel and rebuild.

When I was in the middle of heartache, mourning loss, or facing another unexpected pivot—worship held me together. When I couldn't find the words, the melodies found me. When I didn't have strength, the lyrics lifted me. When all I had was brokenness, worship helped me offer it as a sacrifice.

And to see that same heart for worship in Malia? There are simply no words. As a parent, you dream about your children growing into kind, compassionate, wise people. You pray for their health. Their happiness. Their confidence. You pray for good friends and solid influences. And if faith is important to you, like it is to me— you pray they know God.

But you also know the world has other plans. You know the distractions are loud. The road is full of detours. And there comes a point when you can no longer carry your child's faith for them.

You can only lead them to the water. And force them to drink until they get too old for forcing.

And let me tell you—there were moments Malia took detours. She wrestled. She questioned. She pulled away. She explored. But what gives me peace is knowing that she always returned. Back to God. Back to worship.

Now, as I watch her step into adulthood—her own woman, her own faith, her own walk—I'm undone.

I watch her lift her hands in worship, eyes closed, face lifted toward heaven, and it stops me in my tracks. Because I know—this is not because of me. This is not borrowed faith. This is hers. This is real. And it breathes life into my soul.

There is no greater reward than seeing your child fall in love with the same God who carried you through the darkest parts of your own journey.

Because faith isn't something you inherit. It's something you choose. And watching Malia choose it—over and over again—reminds me that none of it was in vain.

Every whispered prayer over her crib. Every youth night we drove to when we were exhausted. Every Bible verse scribbled on sticky notes and taped to her mirror. Every conversation about right and wrong, love and grace, truth and trust.

None of it returned void. Faith is the reason I'm still standing. Faith is the reason I get up every day and try again. Because I don't know how things will turn out. But I know Who holds the outcome. And that's enough.

I've learned that faith is not the absence of fear. It's choosing to move anyway. It's praying even when you're angry. Worshiping even when you're grieving. Believing even when the odds feel insurmountable.

Faith is asking God to show up—and then making space in your life for Him to move.

Because belief without action? That's just wishful thinking. That's vibes and vision boards with no foundation. You have to move like you believe it. Walk like you expect it. Give like you trust it. And when you fall flat on your face—and I have, many times—then dust yourself off and try again. You can dust it off and try again (ahh the year 2000). Because you know this isn't the end. Because you know God isn't finished.

This chapter of my life—and of our lives—is living proof of that promise. From a confused little girl watching Christmas specials, trying to piece together the story of Jesus... to a mother raising a daughter who worships with abandon and walks with God on her own terms?

That's nothing but God. So thank you, Lord.

For your grace. For your patience. For your covering when I didn't even know I needed it. For your provision in the valley and your presence on the mountaintop.

For holding me and my daughter steady through every storm—and for reminding us, always, that we are never alone.

God, you are faithful. And I am forever grateful.

Malia's Perspective

J esus loves us, this I know, for the Bible tells me so. Little ones to Him belong, They are weak but He is strong. Yes, Jesus loves me!" is the first song I remember learning in Sunday School. Simple but an amazing message—that I am loved! By this man, named Jesus, who loved me and "lived" above me in the clouds. That is vaguely how I thought of Him as a little girl. Someone I thought I could write a letter to (I even tried to mail that letter).

I'd venture to say my journey with God started like it does for many people—at birth. On Sundays as a family—we went to church. I never minded it as a child, with the peppermint candies in the bathrooms and the wide aisles to dance in. There were enough "brothers and sisters" in the church that I thought I could hide my books and Barbies, which I definitely brought with me to nearly every service. That was what church looked like for me, unless I got to go to Sunday School. I loved Sunday School as a little kid. Crafts, snacks, new memory verses, friends—what more can you ask for?

I learned about Jesus and God early on, but you know, beginner steps. VeggieTales? The best way to watch His stories and learn His lessons (if you've never watched VeggieTales, my condolences. Go back to the 1990s-2000s episodes and prepare to be entertained). The first verse I remember memorizing and being very proud of was Psalms 1:1-3. "Blessed is the one who does not walk in step with the wicked, or stand in the way that sinners take, or sit in the company of mockers, but whose delight is in the law of the Lord…" (however I currently cannot say that verse by heart). And the best part of the year? Tying for first place are Christmas festivities and Vacation

Bible School. VBS was my absolute favorite and the closest I got to going to summer camps as a kid. Finding out which color I was in, participating in singing, games, and challenges, and learning a new verse with a keychain each day? I'm a sucker for VBS week. So much so, in fact, that I volunteered to be on staff as soon as I was old enough, for two years.

It wasn't until maybe third or fourth grade that I really started to grasp what was being told to me week after week. Concepts such as Jesus dying for our sins, God having a plan for our lives, and God always being with you. Slowly, the stories I loved as a kid were bigger than the drawings I would see on pages. It really happened, and God is truly our Father in Heaven. I saw no reason to believe otherwise. An eye-opening, but still a very cool idea—that God is with us always and that's what Jesus did for us. Every church service ended the same way, and I was taught that if we want or need something, we need to pray. I prayed at church and with my parents before dinner and bed, but my first time praying on my own was when I started to get bullied.

Getting bullied by your friends is a sick and twisted type of evil; having the girls you viewed as your best friends become the people who would come after you. But I was told I have God on my side, so I went home and I prayed. "God, please make them stop being so mean" or "God, please find me new friends," but back then I thought praying to God was like getting McDonald's. So when He didn't immediately respond to my requests, I was heartbroken. I couldn't understand. I thought God was always with me? I only prayed to God a couple of times, but very quickly, I started to give up on Him. I would attend church every week with my family, and as some of my friends remember, I raised my hand every time a question was asked in Sunday School. But all of that became run-of-the-mill, as I had become confused and frustrated. It didn't feel like God loved me if He wasn't answering me.

As middle school started, I was in the midst of friendships being hard, and I was starting to navigate two very different blended families. Home and school both felt like the Spaceship ride at the fair, spinning and spinning so fast you can't even pick your head up. I was twirling by myself, but thankfully this dredge of feeling alone didn't last long. In sixth grade, you could join the youth group at my dad's church. A simple two hours on Wednesdays where middle schoolers and high schoolers gathered together to play games and learn something about the Lord. It took a while for my shyness to go away, and I could only go every other week for a while, but being a part of that group truly changed my life.

I met new friends that altered everything, and piece by piece, I got to relearn who God is. Through lessons and activities with my group and youth pastors, I became confident in being a daughter of God. He is so intentional, back in Bible days and in the here and now, and younger me started to heal as I saw how God worked and, again, how much He loved me. Even more, I got to do that with amazing people! Youth group was where I learned how important it is to have a community around you to build you up. Having at least fifteen people to talk with as I'm learning and to pray for me was life-giving, and when the Tilt-A-Whirl felt too much, they were there as comfort and support. Worst case, by 6:30 pm, I could take a deep breath and play capture the flag.

I got to go on my first mission trip in 2018 with my youth group to Portland, Oregon, for nine days. During the trip, we had the opportunity to volunteer in a variety of ways, such as cleaning up a school building, working in a senior care garden, and packing food at a food bank. One day, we spent time at a food bank where we learned how to navigate the space and understood the process of distributing food to those in need. Beforehand, the staff informed us that most of the people who came to the food bank were homeless and didn't speak English. I didn't have a direct connection to their experiences, but I wanted to help however I could. Thankfully, we were paired up so that no one would be assisting a guest alone—until near the end of the shift, when an older woman entered while most of my group had stepped out. I volunteered to help her, only to realize that she spoke only Chinese. My nerves flared as I struggled to communicate, using gestures and trial-and-error attempts to explain the process. Despite our language barrier, we slowly found a rhythm, and I was able to guide her through the process of getting the food she needed.

When we finished, I gestured to ask if she wanted help carrying her food, and she nodded. As we walked outside, she passed all the cars, heading toward the street. Confused, I lightly tapped her shoulder, and she pointed ahead. I assumed her car was nearby—until we stopped at a large tree. She turned to me, grinning, and hugged me tightly before unpacking her groceries beneath its branches. It took a moment to register: this tree was her home. Swallowing my shock, I focused on helping her organize her food. When we were done, she embraced me again, radiating warmth and gratitude. Back inside, I sat in quiet reflection. It's one thing to know homelessness exists; it's another to walk someone's groceries to a tree. It was bitter-sweet—heartbreaking, yet she was one of the happiest, most grateful people I'd ever met. As our van pulled away, I saw that she had been joined by a man—maybe her husband or son. She looked up, caught my gaze, and grinned, waving. I teared up as I waved back. That day changed me. That experience showed me that service isn't about being perfect—it's about showing up with a heart willing to help and trusting that, even in moments of struggle, God can work through our efforts to make a difference. That woman, and that moment, was the beginning of my serving heart.

Month after month, one trip after another, my faith and relationship with the Lord grew even stronger. Slowly, I started to integrate the things I had learned and experienced in my everyday life. God was blessing me, my family, and friends, and had brought us so far, I was confident in who God was. But as with every lesson in life, the foundation I had built suddenly started to crumble.

When my family friend passed away from cancer, I couldn't figure out what went wrong. At first, hearing about the sickness didn't bring fear because God knew what was happening. He was in control, and He was going to fix it. He's fixed problems time and time again. So why wouldn't He then? During that time, I remember my dad, stepmom, mom, and everyone in my church communities all urging us to pray to God that He will heal our friend, so that's what I did. I prayed and told others to pray, and quickly my frustration faded. I knew God would fix it.

He passed away at the end of February right before I graduated from high school, and around then, my faith came to a halt. I still went to youth group and church, but for a while, I didn't really believe what I was singing or hearing. My brother had said something back when we were told our friend wasn't going to get better.

"Why isn't God doing anything?" he had said. Well, kind of yelled.

My sadness and anger went back and forth, not sure where to land. Why didn't God heal him? Death took him, and it seemed like God was just "standing" there, watching it happen. Worship, prayer, and faith started to feel meaningless if God wasn't going to be there for us anymore. It reminded me of how I felt in middle school —alone.

But thankfully, having communities that support you in your faith were still standing beside me, and one of the people that shockingly brought me through and out of my crisis of faith was my school counselor. He was reached out to by my family that I was going through a loss, and at first, I treated his questions and my answers like a routine follow-up. But after discovering he was a Christian and had a genuine heart for what I was going through, I came to him with my confusion and told him I was mad at God for doing what He did. My school counselor let the room go silent and let my tears fall before smiling at me.

"Malia, death happens because of the sin in the world," and I can't explain it, but as my tears continued to fall, I felt the most overwhelming sense of peace. As my mom and I like to quote, "lightning just struck my brain."

My counselor explained that while God never intended sickness or death, He is still in control, even when we don't understand. Sometimes He heals, and other times, He brings people home. It hurts because we love them, but God promises to restore everything—no more sickness, no more death. Until then, He is with us, holding us through the pain. Though I was still hurting and didn't understand, my worries eased. As my family traveled to the memorial, I wished him rest and peace. In that moment, I began to piece

225

my faith back together, learning where my strength comes from. Strength, and love, all come from Him.

As my faith was faltering, I was also going through the trying time of applying and deciding which college to go to. I wasn't too sure where I wanted to go, just that I wanted to write. Having a minor setback in discovering that there aren't a ton of Creative Writing programs, I still applied to every college that did. Amongst the colleges that I started to look into was Hamilton College, a private school in Clinton, New York. I don't remember how I found it, but I fell in love with it the second I did. Other than the very hyped-up writing program, I also loved the look of campus, the aesthetic of New York in general, and that Hamilton College is the same name from the amazing musical, *Hamilton.* Now, back then, I didn't understand that those weren't the best reasons for choosing a college—all of New York isn't New York City, and New York is very cold. I hate the cold.

At that point I had University of Colorado - Boulder, University of Denver, and even Colorado University, but I was banking on Hamilton College. I was dreaming of going there, envisioning what my new dorm would look like, and I even started a TikTok to show my outfits leading up to the day I would get my acceptance letter. Overeager is a great phrase to use here. The plan to go to my dream college was all set in stone… until I got rejected from Hamilton College. I cried the rest of that night, and you would've thought I had gotten into a car wreck with how turned around and shocked I felt. This was the end of January, and the only other offers I had were from schools in Colorado that don't have creative writing programs. I love my friends and family, but I couldn't shake the thought that I was suddenly trapped.

A superhero came to my aid, and of course, it was my mom. She told me to go pick out a color scheme for my dorm room, and we set out to start shopping so we could find the joy of going to college again. HomeGoods was the first stop, of course, and it was there that my mom bought me the softest, most comforting plum blanket for my future room. In that thrill, we looked up a dozen more schools to apply to. A list was made, goals were set, and I started applying again. We prayed that I land where God wanted me to, and that it will all come how it was supposed to. Soon enough, I got one, two, three, and more letters of acceptance back. I even got a video from the University of Iowa, personally addressing me to inform me that I had gotten in. But none of these places felt right to me; they just felt like colleges. In my head, time was running out, as it was nearing the end of March. People were making their decisions, and I was falling behind. I wanted a school so perfect for me, like it was written in a book, and that's what God did.

As the letters kept coming, the other big issue was money. I knew we couldn't afford college, but the numbers my family and I were given were jarring, to say the least. Applying for scholarships started to become a daily occurrence, a lot of them being found by my mom. Like I said, superhero. In her search, she looked for scholarships where I could submit a writing piece. If there's anything I could say for people to support my academic advancements, writing would be it. So, she looked and came across an Angie Thomas writers scholarship.

If you don't know the name, Angie Thomas is a bestselling author known for her debut novel, *The Hate U Give*, which follows a Black teenage girl who witnesses the police shooting of her unarmed friend. The book became a cultural phenomenon, earning numerous awards and inspiring a film adaptation. Amazing book, movie, and story. Angie went to a college called Belhaven University, and was in their creative writing program. This scholarship required a portfolio, and the winner would receive a full ride to Belhaven University and into the writing program. When my mom came to me with this scholarship, she had a master plan of her own.

She told me in the car in my dad's driveway, smile and eyes bright with excitement, "I found this writing scholarship from Angie Thomas. You're going to apply to the school and the scholarship, and then we're going to go visit the school." I'm sure I looked at her with a combination of confusion and "absolutely not." She showed me her phone after looking up Belhaven, and my eyes drifted over the pretty campus before stopping at the location.

"Mississippi?"

Imagine that with a disgusted tone, because there was no way I was going there. I've only been to the South a couple of times, but Mississippi, of all places? I was hesitant for sure, but lightning had struck my mom's brain. Actually, bigger than that. She said God had struck her brain, and He was tugging at me now. Coming from a "why not" mentality, I applied for both the school and the scholarship and pretty quickly got connected to an amazing woman in administration who was with my mom and me every step of the way. We found a day we could tour the campus and the program, got the flight tickets, and all we needed was the yes from the school. Days before the flight, we called our administration helper, and she announced to me and my mom that I had gotten into Belhaven! We were thrilled and packed for the trip.

Jackson, Mississippi, is humid, with tons of greenery. Everything looked different and felt different. Excitement and nerves pricked at my heart as we got ready for the tour and the meeting of the professors over the program. Almost instantly, the worries subsided upon meeting one professor who just loves writing and Chick-Fil-A, and the other who was intimidating but in a challenging, encouraging way. I even got to meet other creative writing students and get critiques on my own work. I was so nervous to read my piece aloud, the first step in my writing journey starting then. Up until that point, no one had commented on my work who actually studied writing and knew what was good and what wasn't. So, the validation from both the professors and students made me feel like I could actually pursue what I love. After the first professor pleaded for me to go there, and my mom and I saw a beautiful bookstore, what God had said was pretty much made clear. But usually, what God calls you to do is scary, and by the time we got home, I found myself wanting to say yes to Iowa, not Belhaven. I told my mom that Iowa also had a big writing program, it was closer, and really in my head, it felt easier. Going to Mississippi felt a lot bigger a task than Iowa, and I wasn't ready.

Ironically, my mom told me that that was exactly the reason I had to go. She held me close in my bedroom, pointing at my computer. Iowa had made me a video, sure. But God made an unbelievable path to where He was calling me. From finding the school at the last minute to meeting the professors, hearing their positive feedback on my work, and interacting with the students, it was an overwhelming and affirming experience. All which occurred within just a couple of weeks. And the final nail in the coffin, after we returned, I received an email congratulating me on winning the Angie Thomas Scholarship. Now, I didn't get the full ride, but I did get awarded

$6,000 a year, which is huge! It propelled me forward in such a way that, praise the Lord, my freshman year became free with other scholarships and opportunities. At this point, there were signs and flashing lights and bright fireworks telling me to leave home and become a Blazer.

I decided to commit to Belhaven University, found an amazing roommate, and just a couple of months later, I was packing my bags and flying across the country to start college. I was so excited for all of the friends I was going to meet, my classes, and couldn't wait for the blessings God would give me. Except, they weren't the blessings I thought they would be. My first roommate was a literal disaster, classes were hard, I got stuck with bad group partners or bad grades, and some critiques of my writing were rough and hard to swallow.

Quickly, I was already calling my mom in tears, certain I had made the wrong choice. After multiple new friendships let me down, and classes got harder, when freshman year ended I told my mom I didn't want to go back to Belhaven. I was dreading it, actually. I couldn't see God's bigger picture during that first year, especially since the year after that, my mom and I struggled to find scholarships. God sent me somewhere, and it was hard, and I wanted it to be easy. But during that summer, I looked through photo albums and found something other than heartache and lessons. Suddenly, all of my blessings and joys started to appear.

I met one of my best friends at Belhaven—she was my suitemate. Kind of like a roommate, but the bathroom we shared separated our rooms. It started as knocking on each other's bathroom door, to just barging in, to becoming friends for life. I met her, along with several friends, there, and now I can't imagine life without them. The feedback I found harsh at the beginning grew me into the writer I am today, and I am so proud of how far I've come. One of the biggest blessings of where God called me to be was the church home I discovered once moving to Jackson. I had visited multiple churches, all of them good, but just felt like I was checking "church" off my to-do list. Nothing stuck out to me. At the fifth church I tried, I was welcomed immediately, and during worship, I felt alone with God but also surrounded by so much encouragement and people who needed Him just as much as I did. The sermon was very intentional, not calling me out but calling me up to be more proactive about my relationship with God and with sharing His Word. By the end of the service, I had rededicated my life to the Lord after the rocky year I had and decided that I had found my home church.

God has worked on my heart more than ever before while being there. My serving heart has grown while being in two different serving teams across the church. I've been part of multiple Bible studies with different groups that changed my perspective on following Christ and gave me a community I couldn't have survived college without. I also decided to get baptized again with this church community, which was such an amazing time with a group of people that have become my family.

Iowa would've been easy—and so would a world where my family friend was still here, or where childhood came without the bruises of bullying. But none of that would've helped me grow, and more importantly, none of that would've been from God. It makes me so blessed and honored to be called His daughter.

My life is a living testimony of what God can do, how He orchestrates plans for the bigger picture so that His will is done, and how much He loves us. He is the grand storyteller for all of us, including me and all my blessings in each season. I am honored to know Him as Adonai El Roi, the God who sees me.

"She gave this name to the Lord who spoke to her: 'You are the God who sees me,' for she said, 'I have now seen the One who sees me.'" – Genesis 16:13

"She's my best friend—she's everything to me.
It's always just been me and her against the world."
- Jacquelyn Middleton

CHAPTER NINE

Accomplishments

Olivia's Perspective

There's a certain kind of magic that happens when you see someone else living the way you wish you had the courage to live yourself.

For me, that person has always been Malia.

From the beginning, she has been unapologetically herself. I like to call it "Malia to her core." Authentic. Quirky. Sparkly.

Her "muchness" was impossible to ignore. Even as a toddler, it radiated from her tiny body like glitter from a shaken bottle—loud, colorful, and all over everything. From her expressive eyes and massive smile to her bold fashion choices (that almost always included a tutu or something with pink and an obnoxious amount of sequins), she danced through life like the world was her stage. Literally.

Grocery store aisles, church parking lots, airport terminals—it didn't matter where she was. If a song moved her spirit, she'd break into dance. The epitome of "dance like no one's watching," except everyone *was* watching... and she loved it.

She'd rock messy braids, mismatched socks, a shiny skirt, a rainbow jacket, and a feather in her hair with confidence so pure, it bordered on majestic. Braces? Fabulous. Polka-dot glasses? Iconic. That was Malia—dripping in muchness, glowing with self-love.

She had the confidence I only dreamed of at her age.

When I looked in the mirror as a little girl, I saw a girl that wasn't beautiful. A girl who didn't quite fit in. A girl trying so hard to blend in that she nearly erased herself in the process.

When Malia looked in the mirror, she saw a girl who was fabulous.

And she was right.

I admired that about her—the way she owned herself fully. Even her big feelings. When something upset her, she didn't bottle it up. She didn't shrink. She let the whole house know. One of my favorite Malia quotes of all time came during one of these very passionate moments. Maybe her favorite pink tutu was in the wash, or maybe she couldn't stay up late to read a million books before lights out. Something not too major. But the drama? Legendary. She wailed, "My life is crying!"

That was it. That one line. That was the moment.

And now, nearly two decades later, it's become a family phrase—passed down like an heirloom. Something goes wrong? We say it. Forgot it was National Pizza Day? *"My life is crying."* Get a surprise bill in the mail? *"My life is crying."* It's our comedic shorthand for the inconvenient heartbreaks of adulthood.

That same "muchness" lasted for years, but like it often does for girls, it slowly began to taper off in middle school.

The world got rough. The girls got mean.

They didn't cherish Malia's authenticity like I did. They criticized it. Picked it apart. Mocked her for the very things that made her magical. And over time, she got quiet. She crawled into herself. She dimmed her light just enough to avoid the judgment. She played small so she wouldn't stand out.

It's the same performance so many of us give on a daily basis. Smile when it hurts. Laugh when you're unsure. Shrink to survive. Fit in at all costs.

But slowly, I've seen her finding her way back. Reclaiming those wonderful parts of that confident little girl. Rediscovering the muchness as she steps into womanhood.

And what's beautiful is that she's helping me rediscover mine too.

These days, the roles have started to shift. Malia doesn't just take in the advice I give her—she throws it right back with accuracy and grace.

There are moments, especially in seasons of doubt, where I find myself questioning who I am, what I'm doing, and if I've already lived the best parts of my life. And then here she comes—saying something like, "When you're authentically yourself, your brand has no competition."

Umm… wait! That's my line!

But she's right. She repeats it back to me with full conviction and zero hesitation. Sometimes, hearing your own words reflected back at you is the only way to truly believe them. She says what I need to hear at the exact moment I need to hear it.

Especially now.

There was a time not long ago—after the losses, the grief, the pandemic fog, the burnout—where I knew I needed a change. I was reevaluating everything. Life. Purpose. Career. Identity. For so long, every major decision I made about work had revolved around what others needed from me. I started my business because I needed to be available for my kids. I closed that business and got a full-time job because my family needed the stability.

But now? Now they were older. Now it was about me.

It was Malia who challenged me to think differently. She asked, "What do you want in this next phase of life?" And when I finally had the courage to name it out loud, she looked me dead in the eye and said, "Then go get it."

I didn't want to work for myself anymore. I wanted out of my home office. I wanted to collaborate with people, be part of a team, and help champion a mission bigger than me. So, I started looking.

Opportunities came. I pushed myself to apply for roles that stretched me. And two unique job offers came to the table—both incredible in their own ways.

I was stuck. Torn. Indecisive.

I prayed. But God was no help this time. *"I will be with you regardless of which one you choose,"* He said. Wow, thanks, Lord. For nothing! I appreciate the support, but I need some specifics.

So, I called Malia.

She had just gotten to college and was on the other side of the country. But when I heard her voice answer the phone, I felt like I had already made the right decision—just calling her. *"Moooooo-Leeeee-Ahhhhh!"* I shouted, already feeling better.

I told her everything. The two roles. The mission. The pros and cons. And without skipping a beat, she said, *"It's obvious. You lit up when you talked about the job with students. I could literally hear the smile on your face through the phone. You're meant for this."*

So that was that.

I accepted the role that brought me further into the world of students and education—and it turned out to be one of the best professional decisions I've ever made. I work with the most incredible CEO I've ever worked for. I get to build alongside a phenomenal team. And most of all, I get to wake up every day and pour into a mission that aligns with who I am, what I value, and why I was put on this earth.

And the best part?

It all started with my daughter asking, "But what do YOU want?"

You see, parenting is funny. You spend all those years shaping, teaching, correcting, modeling—and then suddenly, your child becomes your mirror. Your muse. Your advisor. Your accountability partner. Your coach. Your inspiration.

Malia is all of that and more.

She reminds me of who I am and who I still have the power to become.

Her creativity, her brilliance, her emotional intelligence, her "my life is crying" dramatics—they aren't just quirks of personality. They are echoes of her purpose. And they have reflected something back to me that I didn't even know I'd lost.

My muchness.

My own boldness. My joy. My God-given ability to light up a room. To lead. To inspire. To laugh loudly and love hard. And yes... to cry dramatically when necessary.

She has taught me that the courage to be fully yourself is contagious.

And maybe, just maybe, that's the legacy her and I are leaving behind—not just a book, but the reminder that there is power in authenticity.

Malia, to her core, is a masterpiece in progress.

And I am honored—deeply honored—to be a part of her journey.

I admire the way Malia so effortlessly balances organization and creative flow. It's one of the most beautiful and mysterious things I've ever witnessed up close. Honestly, it feels like wizardry.

Controlled chaos.

A symphony of art and precision.

God really knew what He was doing when He gave that girl a generous dose of her dad's obsessive-compulsive habits, sprinkled in with just enough of my freewheeling, last-minute messiness to keep things spicy.

This particular cocktail of traits, while confusing to most people—including me—has served her well. I often find myself standing in awe, watching her move between her worlds. One foot in the clouds, chasing inspiration at 2:00 a.m., and the other firmly planted in color-coded, hyper-detailed reality. I wish I had that kind of balance. I tend to live mostly in the creative ether, floating from idea to idea, grabbing glittering concepts out of thin air but struggling to return them to Earth in a structured way. Malia? She floats too, but then she lands them gracefully in a perfectly formatted spreadsheet. Who does that?

Here's what this magical balance looks like in practice:

Malia will be going about her life, doing the absolute most, as usual—burning a candle at both ends, procrastinating just enough to make your heart skip a beat, staying up all night like it's a creative marathon, and then, somehow, she bangs out something brilliant. Not just "this'll do" good. Brilliant.

I'm talking pure, polished, publishable genius.

Meanwhile, the scene around her looks like a disaster zone, like a tornado touched down right in the middle of her bedroom. There are clothes thrown all over the bed and draped over chairs, books scattered across the floor, loose papers loose, crumpled post-its, tangled charging cords, a trail of snacks, and at least four open notebooks, each containing fragments of stories, ideas, and characters. Somewhere in that hurricane, there's a half-eaten box of Samoas Girl Scout cookies and an empty cup from Dunkin.

She gets this from me. No question.

It's a scene I know well. Creative storm mode. I've lived it for decades and still do.

But just when I start thinking it's gone too far, it happens.

I blink—and the room transforms.

I'm talking pristine. Everything in its place. Not a sock out of line. Not a stray notebook in sight. Bed made. Surfaces wiped. Candles lit. It's giving Pinterest. It's giving "This space is sponsored by The Container Store." It's giving sorcery.

I don't know how she does it. I mean, I know how I sort of try to do it—painfully, and with multiple internal breakdowns before it's ever even close to somewhat clean. But Malia? She makes it look effortless. She has this switch. This "now it's time for structure" gear that she taps into like a seasoned CEO managing a billion dollar corporation and a creative studio at the same time.

She definitely got this part from her dad.

And then—let us not forget—the spreadsheets. Oh, the glorious, insane spreadsheets!

There's one that catalogs her entire book collection—complete with author, genre, rating, and notes. One that tracks her wardrobe inventory down to the accessories. Another that lays out her outfits for each day of the month like a fashion calendar. One that maps out every major school assignment with estimated hours of completion and required research materials. And then there's a series of spreadsheets—yes, a series—dedicated solely to the backstories of the fictional characters in her books. I'm not talking "likes long walks on the beach" kinds of bios. I mean in-depth psychological profiles, generational trauma trees, zodiac signs, Enneagram types, favorite childhood cereal, greatest fears, and relationship timelines.

Scary right?
Who does that?

Malia.

And while the spreadsheets may frighten me a little—they are also glorious. They are brilliant. They are…inspiring.

It's this brilliant combination—her untidy, passionate, whimsical creative side, partnered with her meticulous, organized, detail-loving side—that has not only allowed her to be so successful as a student and a writer, but will absolutely be the thing that propels her into the future she's building. She is a dreamer with a planner. A novelist who understands timelines. She can chase the wind and still file her taxes on time (we hope). She can lose herself in a story while also managing deliverables.

And honestly? That's power.

That's legacy-level power.

Sometimes I stare at her in mid-flow—headphones in, typing furiously on her laptop, tabs open, spreadsheets minimized, a candle burning nearby, snacks within arm's reach, a sticky note on her mirror that says something like "You're fabulous," and I just think to myself:

I did that. God did that. But also… I did that!

She is what happens when all the best parts of two people show up in the same body—and somehow make it work.

And maybe it's not effortless for her. Maybe it just looks that way because she's learned how to lean into both sides of herself. But to me, as her mom watching from the sidelines, it feels like a masterclass in how to be both/and in a world that constantly demands either/or.

She embraces the contradiction, turns it into her superpower, and leaves everyone else wondering how she manages to make it look so beautiful.

And that? That's the part that leaves me breathless.

She is the accomplishment I'm most proud of.

Malia's Perspective

There are three photos of my mom that are my favorite. For one of them, I'm not sure why I have it or how I got it, but it sits in my Google Drive, ready to be admired again. In it, she has on the iconic black glasses, her amazing smile, and what looks to be a superhero symbol. Probably DIY, like all things in the house, it was a Wonder Woman tiara, sometimes functioning as a weapon, like a boomerang. It is a yellow triangle with a red star in the center, and my mom wore it triumphantly. That is who she is. My mom is Wonder Woman.

A lot of what I adore—not just admire—about my mom, I didn't get to see until I was older. As the picture of her life got bigger, I got to rediscover all the amazing things about my mom that I just couldn't fully see as a child. Especially when I wouldn't stop twirling around to music in different dresses. Which brings me to the first of many things I admire about my mom: the way she cares for the people around her. Whether that be me and my brother, her mom, her coworkers, her friends, or her family, over the years, I got to watch her intentionality with other people. There was so much love that she poured into the things she did for others or the events she would do with others. Whether it be church or her friend group that I was obsessed with, she didn't do anything without thinking of them. Even in helping me with my gifts to friends, she showed me through her actions that the thought you put into caring for the people you love is of the utmost importance. But her biggest acts of care came from places where her bucket wasn't full.

It started first with me and my brother. During elementary school and into middle school, time at her house felt so magical. She cast me and my brother in multiple videos, our biggest hits being our chaotic cooking video and us trying to say Werther's caramel correctly. There was a partially broken disco ball that hung in the "dining" room, and the three of us would have a dance party almost every night. During the holidays, we would decorate our baby tree, and a cute little elf would suddenly appear. Kids reading, close your eyes here—but my mom would move our elf around so we could scream and freak out all over again in the morning. I had several sleepovers in that house with the help of my mom, and she had a sleepy pillow mist or Celestial Sleepy Time Tea at night and our good morning songs ready for school the next day. I remember these memories as some of the best times of my life—of our lives—but that was living inside this beautiful picture. I have stepped outside of it and realized that it wasn't always the best time for my mom.

During all of this, she was a single mom with a full-time, demanding job, along with all the other hardships that life hands us. In our conversations now, she's told me that she sometimes had to force herself to do those videos, and spending time on that dang elf was not fun at all. Christmas wasn't a holiday my mom enjoyed, but we decorated, opened gifts, and listened to Christmas music anyway. From dance parties to Halloween outfits, those memories hold some weight with joy—weight that my brother and I didn't see. We weren't supposed to. I know that moms put aside their feelings and jobs for their children and do things to create memories, but moms don't have to. My mom didn't have to. Who needs a cooking video where I'm stuttering like nobody's business and my brother is saying his name backwards?

For my mom and all moms out there, it is not talked about enough—the time, emotion, and tiredness that are put to the side in order to create memories for their children that will never be forgotten. That is a decision and dedication that doesn't go unnoticed. Some of my favorite moments from my childhood exist in the seasons of your hardships and real emotion. So, Mom, truly, thank you. That is a strength and love that I hope to carry.

My second favorite photo of my mom was taken on April 24, 2024, but I didn't receive it until weeks later. It was a picture of my mom the day she visited my college church in Jackson, Mississippi. She has her eyes closed, arm raised, and is deeply engaged in a moment of worship. She has short, natural hair and is wearing a denim jacket over a dark-colored shirt. She is holding a coffee cup in her other hand (of course) and is fully immersed in God's presence. Throughout my life, I have gotten a front-row seat to my mom's relationship with God, and it has been an amazing inspiration to my own walk with Christ.

Prayer and church were exposed to me basically at birth, and attending service with my mom quickly became routine. But God's presence went past those four walls. Worship played throughout the house, my brother and I would play through the pews on the weekends, and we watched Mom at dance practice. Even as a kid, I got to see my mom's relationship with God flow into every area of her life, which flowed into my own. My foundation of praying, praising, and my own faith was built off of seeing my mom experience God. Watching her worship her Savior is a beautiful sight to see. I have been in awe, watching my mom. Her commitment to her relationship brought me to dive into my faith, understanding and believing what my mom did. From Sunday School to standing next to her in service, how she made her way in life as a follower of Christ allowed me to see her more clearly. It lets me celebrate my mom's flaws and my own and lean on the One that she leans on. Getting to see her worship bloom and grow has been beautiful.

My third favorite photo of my mom isn't just one—it's a collection of moments. It's her smile, her outfit, the way she adjusts her glasses, and the ever-changing set of slides she flips through every time she gives a speech. It's the way her entire presence shifts, glowing with energy, her eyes twinkling like never before. As I grew up, I got to witness her inner passions come to life on stage. It was almost like she became someone else—not a different person, but a bolder, amplified version of herself. Her words became louder, her statements sharper, and her laughter even bigger.

Over the years, my mom would take me to many of these speeches, and every time, I got to watch her not only grab the attention of her audience but invite them into her world. It never felt forced—she had a way of making people feel like they belonged in the conversation, like they were in on something special. When I was younger, I was mesmerized by the way she commanded a room, how people hung onto every word. But as I got older, I became less focused on what she was saying and more in awe of how she said it. I fell in love with her passion. With every speech, every impassioned explanation, every moment she shared her knowledge, I saw the fire in her. And I want that fire for myself.

I want to be like my mom when I grow up. Not just in the way she stood tall in front of a room or in the way she always had the perfect words ready, but in the way she poured herself into her work. Her job isn't just a job—it's a calling, a gift, something she carries with her every day. She doesn't just present ideas; she breathes life into them. It never fails—after she's done speaking, someone always comes up to her, eager to share how much her words meant to them. It makes me think that her speeches aren't just presentations; they're introductions to who she is. More than a product, more than a service, more than an idea—her work is a reflection of the artist behind it.

If I'm with my mom when she's heading out for a speech, I find myself just as excited as she is—thrilled, once again, to watch her step into her element, to see her ignite a room full of people with her fiery passion. And she's damn good at it.

She was so good at what she did that one day, I bounced into her room, barely able to contain my excitement over an announcement. I wasn't at the age where I could fully mess up the bed, but when I crawled over to her, I made my presence known.

My mom looked at me with a wild, almost crazy look in her eyes and said, "I'm going to write a book."

At the time, I was working on my second book, and I couldn't fully process what she was trying to tell me. She was going to write a book? My mom? I blinked at her, waiting for her to elaborate, and then she grinned madly, explaining that it would be about marketing, about branding—especially for women her age. It took seconds for my initial confusion to turn into absolute joy. We could be authors together!

From that moment on, my mom started writing, and I became her biggest cheerleader. Every single day, I asked how the book was going. I didn't mean to be annoying or to rush the process, but I was desperate to hold her work in my hands. I knew what she was capable of. I knew her passion. I knew the fire that ignited every time she spoke about branding, marketing, and the importance of women owning their stories. And now, she was going to put it all into a book? It was like watching her bottle up all the magic I had seen her share on stage and pour it onto the page.

Day in and day out, for a year, I asked about her book. Every time, she told me she was still working on it. I knew writing a book is no small feat—it's not just about putting words on paper; it's about putting yourself on paper. And my mom wasn't one to do anything halfway.

Then, one day, she finally said the words I had been waiting for: "The book is done!"

I practically screamed. She asked me to help with the illustrations, and I couldn't have been more honored. Working alongside her, watching her project come to life, was something I will never forget. And soon enough, the book was physically in her hands.

I cannot begin to explain how much I admire my mom for this labor, this heart, this project of hers. Writing a book is not just an achievement—it's an act of vulnerability, of courage, of sheer willpower. It's putting your wisdom and your wounds into words and hoping they resonate with someone else.

And the best part? The book came out shortly after mine. We got to celebrate together—mother and daughter, side by side, both published authors. It was a joy so deep, so surreal, that I never want to forget it.

A lot of my own accomplishments come from the reading and writing world—my soul is planted among pages, and it has been for as long as I can remember. My first big accomplishment happened in elementary school when a little dream turned into reality.

In fifth grade, we had designated moments to read every day, but they were always too short. One day, I was body-deep in a book—*Mockingjay* from *The Hunger Games* series, to be specific—when our teacher told us it was time to stop. I groaned loudly, reluctantly closing my book and dragging myself back to my chair. Why couldn't we just read all day? Seriously, why? One day where math and science could be set aside so that every student—not just me—could escape into stories and explore worlds beyond the classroom. Reading was important, after all.

That's when I had a crazy idea. If anyone could make this happen, it would be the principal.

Over winter break, I sat down at the computer and typed out an email, as professional as ten-year-old me could get, asking for a whole day dedicated to reading. I hit send, hopeful but not expecting much.

When school was back in session, my principal came and found me. He said that some tweaks had to be made—seven straight hours of reading wasn't possible—but he liked my idea. We could work with it. I was thrilled! No way was this actually happening.

Over the next few months, I sat with my teacher and principal, ironing out the details. It couldn't be just reading, but it could be a day where the whole school focused on and celebrated literacy. We would still have classes, but throughout the day, the principal would make an announcement, and everyone—students and teachers alike—would stop what they were doing and read! Students could wear their pajamas, and parents would be invited to come in and read to classrooms.

I was over the moon. I couldn't believe what I was hearing!

A few weeks passed, and then it was official. Literacy Day. Set for the end of March.

On the big day, I was asked to give a speech at the assembly, explaining what the day was and why I had pushed for it. I don't remember exactly what I said—just that I loved reading and that it mattered. That was enough.

That day, I was given an award before we all ran off to do what I adored—reading!

From sixth to eighth grade, Literacy Day became an annual tradition, and each year, I kicked it off with a speech. Younger students would join bigger students so they could read together, and one year, I read Spanish books to little kids during my Spanish class. When my book was published, I got to bring it to the assembly as well, standing in front of my classmates with proof that stories could take you far. Freshman year of high school, they invited me back to speak again.

I don't know if they still do Literacy Day. I hope they do. But even if they don't, it's okay.

Because for a while, I got to make a change—for myself and for my classmates. And I got to celebrate the thing that has always brought me joy.

Reading has taken me so far, but through all those adventures, it has led me to the greatest adventure of all—becoming a writer.

Discovering that I could create worlds, express what needed to be expressed, and explore ideas in a way that felt limitless opened a door that can never be closed. I see my entire world through the lens of a writer—who the character is, their arc, their community, the plot, the twists, the purpose—on and on and on. Everything is a story waiting to be told.

When my fingers fly across the keyboard, they don't stop. My imagination unfolds before my eyes, turning thoughts into sentences, sentences into pages, and pages into something real. Finding a way to breathe life into my ideas—the things I want to say, the stories I want to tell, the worlds I want to explore—has been the greatest honor and reward.

And what I have gained from writing isn't money or fame. It's a connection.

My favorite moments as an author have nothing to do with sales or prices. They happen in conversations, in the ways people respond to my stories. Talking with adults about my dreams and passions, hearing from kids who saw themselves in my work, or inspiring a child to enjoy reading—those are my "I did it" moments.

Because it's not just about sharing a piece of myself with the world—it's about the world receiving it. Loving it. Seeing themselves in it.

That's what makes it real.

There will never be a moment more fulfilling than watching a little boy in a wheelchair zoom across the floor, nearly knocking people over to get to his mom so he can have the next book in my series. That's joy. That's the impact. That's why I write.

Or when little girls hand me drawings of their books and their dreams, their eyes wide as they tell me they want to be like me when they grow up—that is all the validation I will ever need.

To know that my work, my ideas, my words hold value. To know that stories—my stories—can change something in someone else.

That will always mean more than any trophy, award, or plaque.

Writing has given me a sense of purpose, a way to connect with others, and the confidence to share my voice with the world. It was proof that I could dream, create, and accomplish something meaningful. But as high school drew to a close, I started to realize that, just like finishing a book, reaching the end of this chapter came with both excitement and uncertainty.

I really don't think you can truly understand or value a season until it's about to close. That's how I felt in my final moments before graduating high school. I was thrilled to finally be at the finish line, but it all felt so surreal. I had felt like just moments earlier, I had been nervously picking out my outfit for the first day of freshman year, having no idea where to go and zero friends—other than that one math teacher with the same last name as me—my dad. And suddenly, I was collecting my things, getting a cap and gown, and being instructed to walk across a stage. Well, a football field—thank you, COVID-19.

High school was a wild time for multiple reasons, the main one being that the student who entered those doors wasn't the same student who walked out of them. The student who walked in had no idea how to earn a grade, let alone grasp the lessons being taught. I was figuring out where writing would take me, uncertain of how I would grow. But over four years as a Raptor, I was forced to become a student—to study subjects, to wrestle with not knowing the answers, and to navigate the struggles of learning.

I stumbled my way into Yearbook, which became my favorite part of high school and allowed me to hone my craft in my greatest joy: storytelling.

I became a leader, with all the highs and lows, and I discovered who I was as a leader in my day-to-day life. And with the honors diploma and everything else, God decided to throw in an extra challenge—a worldwide pandemic. COVID-19 abruptly ended my junior year and more or less ruined my senior year, something that was definitely not on my vision board. Honestly, I kind of crawled my way to the finish line. But the person who came out of it was so much stronger, braver, and more humbled by what I had access to as a student and by the endless things I could learn if I put in the effort.

Receiving my cords for journalism and, shockingly, my GPA felt like a greater celebration of my strides than anything else. High school graduation showed me that I could make my way in the world if I searched, chased, and worked for it.

And along with crossing that finish line, what made it all worth it was celebrating with my family—acknowledging just how far I had come. My mom, dad, stepmom, both of my grandmas, my siblings—everyone surrounding me with love and cheers! Having a support team like them during the journey and afterward was the greatest gift and blessing. They got to watch me grow up, stumble, learn, and ultimately become the person who was moving the tassel over. And in that moment, I wasn't just proud of myself—I was grateful.

Looking back, those four years weren't just about academics or even the friendships I made along the way. They were about growth—about becoming someone who understood the value of hard work, resilience, and passion. High school wasn't easy, but it gave me so much: the space to develop my writing, the opportunity to lead, and the realization that I had a voice worth sharing.

And as I stood in that cap and gown, diploma in hand, I knew this was only the beginning.

The next chapter was waiting to be written.

"Yes, Mother...I can see you are flawed.
You have not hidden it.
That is your greatest gift to me."
- Alice Walker

CHAPTER TEN

Advice

Olivia's Perspective

Dear Malia,

This is for you and for every daughter reading this. I know you sometimes roll your eyes at my unsolicited advice, and I know sometimes you think I'm being dramatic (which, let's be real, I can be - like daughter, like mother). But hear me out—this chapter is for you. For the version of you who thought she had life figured out in her teenage years, for the version of you who will question everything in your twenties, and for the version of you who will look back one day and laugh at what she thought she knew in her thirties.

At the end of the day, you have made me wiser and have given me some of the best advice I've ever received. Being your mom has taught me so much and watching you live your life thus far has completely shifted my perspective on how I live mine. Let's be clear—

I don't have all the answers. I never have. But I've lived long enough to gather a few gems, to take some hard knocks, to love and lose and love and lose and try again. I've seen life turn upside down and back around, and through it all, I've learned a few things that I wish I had known earlier. So here it is—wisdom from a woman who has been through it all, seen it all, made some mistakes, learned some lessons, and is still figuring things out along the way.

You don't have to have it all figured out (seriously, you don't). I know the world makes it seem like you have to have a plan, especially as you embark on adulthood after college. Like you need to map out your entire life, make the right decisions, pick the right career, find the right person, and somehow, magically, never mess up. That's a lie. If everyone has imposter syndrome (which we do) that means no one has it. The truth is, nobody actually knows what they're doing. Even the people who look like they have it all together? They're winging it too—one of my best skills!

You don't have to know all the answers right now. You don't have to decide today what you'll be doing in 10 years because every 10 years it will inevitably change. Just pick a direction and move. For now. Try things. Experiment. Say yes to an opportunity, and if it doesn't work out, say yes to something else. There is no rule that says you have to stick with the first thing you land on. Pivot, change course, pivot again, reinvent yourself and your brand as many times as you need. The people who seem to have the most fulfilling lives? They aren't the ones who knew their path from day one. They're the ones who weren't afraid to change paths, to try, fail, and try again. And if anyone makes you feel like you're behind, remind them (and yourself) that life is not a race.

You are not your mistakes (not even the really ridiculous ones). At some point, you're going to mess up. You're going to make bad choices, trust the wrong people, embarrass yourself, and wonder how you let things get so far off track. Welcome to being human. Failing doesn't make you a failure. It means you're adventurous! There is a huge difference between making a mistake and being a mistake. Between falling down and staying down.

I've often carried my mistakes like luggage—big, heavy, exhausting. If I can't unsee them or let them go then no one else can. I let them define me, haunt me, and make me feel like I wasn't worthy of good things. But here's what I want you to remember: You are always worthy of good things. No mistake is so big that it disqualifies you from love, from success, from joy. You are allowed to mess up. You are also allowed to forgive yourself when you do.

As hard as I may be and as bad as I can be at this, be present. This life is fleeting. When people in my life told me to slow down more and stop putting so much on my plate, I wish I had listened. Don't rush to the next big thing, the next goal, the next milestone. Because life moves fast, and if you're not careful, you'll miss it. I want you to be present. Not just physically, but fully. Enjoy the small moments—laugh so hard that your stomach hurts, quote lots of movies and song lyrics, go on early morning walks, sit outside with a cup of coffee on a quiet morning, feel the sun on your face, get up and dance whenever and wherever music moves you. Time flies less the more present you are. And the more present you are the more you will remember. And one day, when you're looking back, you'll be grateful for every second you actually lived instead of just the ones captured on social media.

The woman you are today is not the woman you will be tomorrow. You are still becoming and will forever be evolving to be better, stronger, and more authentic. The woman you are today will not be the woman you are in five years, or ten, or twenty. And that is beautiful. You are meant to shift and change. You are meant to change your mind, to outgrow places, people, and mindsets that no longer serve you. So don't hold on too tightly to any one version of yourself. Give yourself permission to grow, to bloom in ways you never expected.

Build your "No" muscle. Use it often. Because saying no is hard. Especially at first. But learning to say no is one of the most powerful skills you will ever have. Start small—say no to things that drain you, that don't align with your values, that don't bring you joy. The more you do it, the stronger your "no" muscle gets. Because one day, you're going to have to say a big no—the kind that protects your boundaries, your body, your peace. And I want you to be ready.

Saying no doesn't make you difficult or selfish, less caring or giving. This is what I used to believe. It makes you healthy and whole. Which in turn helps those around you be whole as well.

Embrace your feminine power because as much as I've thought the opposite, softness is not weakness. For so long, I thought I had to do everything myself. Be strong. Be independent. Never need anyone. I let my hyper-independence and desperate need to protect my emotions take over because I thought control meant safety. It took me years to realize that being soft is not the same as being weak. And now it's taking even more years to put this into practice. It's beyond hard to say the least. You don't have to prove your strength by doing everything alone. You don't have to carry the world on your back

262

just to show that you can. Your feminine power is wisdom, intuition, and grace. You are allowed to be cared for. You are allowed to receive help, to rest, to trust, to lean into your softness without fear. That is power too.

Lastly, when life gets messy, focus on what's true. When things get muddy, when you feel lost, when the world feels like it's spinning too fast, I want you to stop and write down the "five things you know for sure". This has saved me in some of the most tumultuous times of my life. They become your anchors. The truths that do not change, no matter how chaotic life gets. In this moment, here's what I know for sure:

1. Each day is a gift.
2. You are amazing.
3. You will be okay.
4. I love you.
5. God's got you.

If you ever feel lost, stand on these things. They will hold you steady.

I don't expect you to take all of this advice in at once. You'll come back to it when you need it. Maybe in a year, maybe in five. But when you do, I want you to hear my voice in your head, reminding you that you are capable, strong, worthy, and so deeply loved. And no matter where life takes you, I will always, always be in your corner.

With all my love and all I am,
Mom

Malia's Thoughts

Dear Mom,

One of the biggest pieces of advice I ever gave you was when you called me about a job decision, back in my freshman year of college. When I saw your name on my phone, I got so excited, thrilled to hear your voice. After catching up, you filled me in on two job offers. One was a job that paid well, a company and team you knew well—it felt almost like a safer option. The other job offer didn't pay as much; it was a new type of job with people you didn't know as well. The riskier job.

You weren't sure which one to pick, but I heard your voice when you told me the options. Your passion was ignited when talking about the risk, and I could see your eyes sparkling in my mind. Almost instantly, I told you to go towards the riskier job. You asked if I was sure, and I said yes—it's the job you want. You'll love it. The doubt crept into your voice then, worried about things like me, my brother, and other people, and I stopped that really quickly.

"Mom, me and my brother are fine. Everyone is fine. Now is the time to take the job you want. Do what you want to do."

After more nerves and excitement were passed over the phone, my mom took the risky job offer, which quickly became a job she loved. Meaning, I give the best advice. I'm kidding—you do, but if I can, let me try to give you some more advice as we step in our new seasons. I have seen you pour yourself into everyone around you, ensuring that every detail is perfect, every person is comforted, and every need is met. From planning weddings to organizing memorials, from preparing meals to handling every behind-the-scenes task, you've made sure the world around you runs smoothly. But, Mom, I want you to know that you deserve the same care and attention that you so willingly give to others.

I think about the events where I've seen you tirelessly working in the background, never taking a seat, never allowing yourself to fully enjoy the moments you've helped create. I hate the times I see you drained, pushing through exhaustion because someone else needs something. Even for me and my brother, you've always been there—giving, providing, making sure we have everything we need. And I cannot explain how grateful we, and everyone in your life, are grateful for how you show up for us. But what I want, more than anything, is for you to do things for yourself. To take the time to live the amazing life you've built!

So, Mom, enjoy events. Sit at the table. Dance your heart out at a wedding. Take trips just because you want to. Experience the world without feeling like you have to be responsible for it. The love you pour into others is beautiful, but you can only pour for so long without refilling your own cup. And I know I struggle with this too, so let's work on it together. Let's both learn to say no when we need to, and yes when it comes to our own joy.

I also want you to remember that your worth is not measured by how much you do for others. There is no scale that evaluates what all you've accomplished to make other's lives better. Your ability to bring people together, to create beauty in the lives of those around you, is a gift. But it should not come at the cost of your own well-being. When you take time for yourself, you are not being selfish—

you are honoring the life that God has given you. The time He has given you to embrace what He has made!

You have spent your life being the giver—the provider of comfort, support, and wisdom. But, Mom, I want you to know that it's okay to be on the receiving end too. Let people love you the way you love them! Let them show up for you without feeling the need to repay them immediately. You are not just valuable because of what you do for others; you are valuable simply because you are you. You have carried so much weight for so many people, often without complaint. But I want you to know that you don't have to carry it alone. The same way you rush to take care of others, allow others to rush to take care of you. Let yourself be nurtured, be celebrated, and be cared for. If you need help, say yes to the first helping hand. Let others support you, accept help without guilt, and embrace love without hesitation. You have given so much—it's time for you to receive.

I know that being vulnerable and allowing others to care for you may feel weird. You've spent so long being strong, independent, and self-sufficient that leaning on others might seem like an impossible task. But strength is not just in giving; it is also in receiving. Let people pour into you the way you have poured into them. And beyond just accepting help, I want you to embrace the love that surrounds you. Let yourself be seen. Let yourself be celebrated. You are not just a support system for others—you are a radiant, dynamic woman (big time magazine editor) who deserves to be uplifted in the same way you have uplifted so many. I know you. I know that your to-do list never seems to end, and I know that you push yourself beyond exhaustion because there's always something to be done. But rest is not a luxury—it's a necessity. And more importantly, resting does not mean you are weak, or lazy, or neglecting responsibilities. It means you are human.

You deserve lazy days. You deserve naps in the middle of the afternoon, books that are read just for fun, and weekends where nothing is planned. You deserve moments where you do absolutely nothing and are in complete bliss about it. So, please, prioritize your rest the way you prioritize everyone else's needs. Know that the world will keep spinning even if you take a break. And I promise you, unfortunately, the work will still be there when you're ready— but you'll be better equipped to handle it when you're well-rested and full of energy, instead of drained and running on empty.

Rest is not just about sleep—it's about renewal. It's about doing things that restore your spirit, whether that's listening to your favorite music, sitting outside in the sun, or taking a quiet moment for prayer and reflection. Sit beside the window in the morning and soak in all that you have, are capable of, and the gifts God gave you. Take a deep breath in, and breathe out. Smile, stretch, take it all in. Your soul deserves rest just as much as your body does.

You have spent so much time making sure others succeed, but I want to make sure you never stop chasing your own dreams. There are still things in this world that are meant for you to experience, create, and accomplish. Whatever dreams you have tucked away, whatever passions you've placed on the back burner—I hope you bring them to the forefront. I am so proud of you for pushing past your obstacles and getting your masters, getting it truly because you want it and need it for what you want to do next in your career.

You have always been creative, always been a visionary. Your ideas, your skills, your passions—they matter just as much as anyone else's. Whether it's starting a new project, or diving into something just because it brings you joy, I hope you never let go of the things that set your soul on fire.

I know life has required you to be practical and responsible. Money is a thing, and children, and needing a job is all very real. But I also know that your dreams are still alive within you. So go after them. Chase them fearlessly. Because you are not just here to help others build their dreams—you are here to live out your own, too. That Barbie job you applied for? Apply for another one! Who knows where your dreams will take you next if you listen to them.

While some dreams like working at Mattel require moves and a different lifestyle, I also want you to know that pursuing your dreams does not have to mean making grand, life-altering changes. It can be as simple as carving out time for yourself to do something you love. It can be taking a step in a direction you've always wanted to go, no matter how small. The point is that you deserve to continue growing, evolving, and experiencing life in a way that fulfills you. There is no glass ceiling when it comes to what you want to accomplish.

Mom, you have always been the one to extend grace, to remind others that they are enough, that mistakes do not define them. But I want you to give yourself that same grace. You don't have to be perfect. You don't have to have it all figured out. You don't have to hold everything together all the time. It's okay to not have all the answers. Everyone makes mistakes, I should know, Hannah Montana taught me that. It is okay to take a deep breath and just be.

I never want you to doubt yourself. You are wise, strong, and full of so much goodness. You've taught me that failing doesn't mean the journey is over, and yet, I know there are times when you hold yourself to a standard of perfection that is impossible to reach. I hope you learn to be as kind to yourself as you are to others. To love yourself through the difficult moments, just as you love me when I struggle. You are already enough—just as you are.

Lastly, Mom, I want you to know that joy is not something you have to earn. You deserve joy simply because you exist. So keep dancing in the kitchen. Keep twirling like your disco balls. Keep laughing loudly, wearing all the colors, and letting your afro run free. You are at your best when you are fully and unapologetically yourself. You are the best version of yourself when you stay true to how God made you. The treasured pieces that make you you is how so many people have found their calling, how some people have thrived in their business and personal brands, and how others have found their faith in Christ. You being you was what allowed me and my brother to grow into the people we are today. So don't limit yourself, ever. Bring all of you to the table because all of it is worth sharing. The light you bring to the world is unmatched, and there are so many people out there who still need to hear what you have to say. I, personally, have learned so much from just being in your presence and there is so much more I want to learn! Your light is powerful, your presence is inspiring, and the world is better because you are in it.

As you know well, when you are yourself there is no competition.

I love you more than words can say.

With all my love,
Malia

Olivia at her Strawberry Shortcake themed 3rd birthday party

Olivia's 1st grade class and the boy in the green overalls

Olivia on Halloween with her hair out for the first time

Olivia, Olivia's dad's mom, and Olivia's mom

Olivia's college graduation after receiving leadership award

New mom Olivia and 2-month-old Malia

Grandma and Malia on their birthday

Malia, Olivia, and her son Gabe

Malia, Gabe, and Olivia's dad Trialfa

Malia after her first dance recital

Olivia and all seven of her younger sisters

Barbies from left to right: Jasmine, Caroline, Sara, Kayley, Katie,
and Ken at church with Malia

Olivia, Malia, and Malia's stepmom Jamie on Malia's birthday

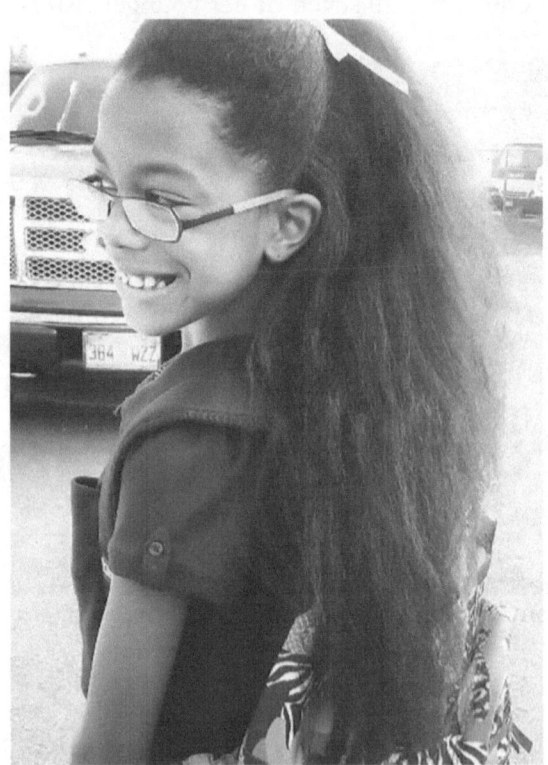

The first time Malia went to school with her hair out

Four generations of daughters: Malia, Grandma, Olivia and Great Grandma T

Malia's first time in a blazer and heels with Olivia

Olivia and Malia's first book signing together

Malia and her four fantasy mystery novels for middle schoolers

Malia and Grandma at her 70th birthday party

Malia's stepmom Jamie, Malia, Olivia, and Grandma at Malia's 18th birthday surprise

Olivia, Malia, Malia's stepmom and dad at Malia's high school graduation party

Malia and Malia's dad's mom Grandma Jane at Malia's graduation

Malia and Olivia at Malia's college church, CityHeart

Olivia worshipping at Malia's college church, CityHeart

Olivia and Malia on the first day of school at Belhaven University

Malia with her family (dad, stepmom, and brothers)

Malia and Olivia graduating from Belhaven University together

ACKNOWLEDGEMENTS

This book is more than words on a page—it is a reflection of the lives, love, and wisdom of those who have shaped us.

Writing *Through Her Eyes* has been a deeply personal journey, one that would not have been possible without the unwavering support, encouragement, and prayers of so many.

To our family, friends, and every person who has played a role in our lives—thank you for the moments, big and small, that became the foundation of these stories.

You are woven into these pages in ways seen and unseen.

To Malia's professors at Belhaven University, thank you for nurturing her creativity, sharpening her voice, and encouraging her to embrace storytelling as a powerful tool for impact. Your guidance and belief in her talent have made an immeasurable difference.

To those who have prayed for us—your faith has lifted us, covered us, and carried us through this process. Your words of encouragement, your belief in this project, and your willingness to intercede on our behalf have meant more than we can express.

We have felt those prayers in moments of exhaustion, doubt, and joy alike, and we are grateful beyond measure.

To everyone who poured into us and believed in this project— your encouragement fueled us when doubt crept in, and your excitement reminded us why this story matters.

You have been our sounding boards, our prayer warriors, and our biggest cheerleaders.

And most of all, to the women who came before us—our mothers, grandmothers, and great-grandmothers—this book is, in many ways, your legacy. Your resilience, courage, and love run through every chapter, every sentence, every word.

Your voices echo in ours.

ABOUT THE AUTHORS

Malia Logan is the author of *The Death Call*, an adventure thriller mystery series for preteens. This four-novel series takes curious readers on a suspenseful journey with Melissa and her middle school friends as they unravel mysteries and face exciting challenges. Malia's creativity is fueled by her boundless imagination and her deep love of reading. She draws inspiration from her favorite authors, including J.K. Rowling (Harry Potter), Angie Thomas (The Hate U Give), and V.E. Schwab (The Invisible Life of Addie LaRue).

Malia began writing her first thriller novel in the 7th grade and has since honed her craft, developing her unique voice and style. She earned a Bachelor of Fine Arts in Creative Writing, with minors in Biblical Studies and Business Administration from Belhaven University in Jackson, Mississippi. Angie Thomas, one of Malia's literary inspirations, is also a Belhaven University alumna and was a part of the same Creative Writing program.

As an Angie Thomas Scholar, Malia has worked to grow her skills across genres, formats, and styles, adding humor, flair, and excitement to both her fiction and nonfiction work. Malia dreams of creating more captivating stories, introducing readers to new characters, and taking them on unforgettable adventures. She aspires to become a world-renowned author and hopes to inspire kids everywhere to pursue their wildest dreams.

Olivia Omega is a branding strategist and seasoned entrepreneur with over 20 years of brand positioning, digital marketing, communications, and advertising experience across startup, nonprofit, public, and private sectors. She is currently the Senior Director of Marketing and Communications at the nonprofit Denver Scholarship Foundation which helps make college possible for Denver students.

As a TEDx speaker, diversity and inclusion advocate, and author, Olivia has studied the importance of authenticity for both brands and individuals and what it means to show up in a genuine way. Half of her career was spent at an advertising agency and the other 10 years as an entrepreneur and small business owner. Personal brand identity and authentic expression of one's unique individuality played a large role in both career paths as described in her book *Beautifully Branded: The Girl's Guide to Understanding the Anatomy of Brand You*.

Olivia graduated from the University of Colorado Boulder Leeds School of Business with a degree in Marketing and earned an MBA in Entrepreneurship from Belhaven University. Olivia volunteers her time mentoring students and lecturing on personal branding and marketing. She has a deep passion for encouraging and inspiring high school and college students in the areas of leadership and business, as well as championing nonprofit projects and missions that elevate under-represented communities.

www.ingramcontent.com/pod-product-compliance
Lightning Source LLC
Chambersburg PA
CBHW021218130626
46554CB00004B/1259